Spiritual Journaling

Spiritual Journaling

Writing Your Way to Independence

Julie Tallard Johnson

Bindu Books
Rochester, Vermont

Bindu Books
One Park Street
Rochester, Vermont 05767
www.InnerTraditions.com

Bindu Books is a division of Inner Traditions International

Library of Congress Cataloging-in-Publication Data
Johnson, Julie Tallard.
  Spiritual journaling : writing your way to independence / Julie Tallard
Johnson.
   p. cm.
  Includes bibliographical references and index.
  ISBN 1-59477-056-5
  1. Teenagers--Religious life. 2. Spiritual journals--Authorship.
  I. Title.
  BL625.47.J62 2006
  204'.46--dc22
                                                              2005028837

Printed and bound in Canada by Transcontinental Printing

10 9 8 7 6 5 4 3 2 1

Text design by Jon Desautels and layout by Priscilla Baker
This book was typeset in Veljovic and Avenir, with Party, Skippy, and Alexa used as display typefaces

"At the Un-national Monument along the Canadian Border" and "The Way It Is" copyright 1975, 1998 by the Estate of William Stafford. Reprinted from *The Way It Is: New & Selected Poems* with the permission of Graywolf Press, Saint Paul, Minnesota.

To send correspondence to the author of this book, mail a first class letter to the author c/o Inner Traditions • Bear & Company, One Park Street, Rochester, VT 05767, and we will forward the communication.

Contents

This book is dedicated to Michele Belisle and Vickie Trihy,
who remind me why I write
and why I keep opening my heart.
Thank you.

Acknowledgments

I am grateful for all the teen voices, named and unnamed, that are found within these pages. Your voice is the medicine we all need.

I offer special thanks to the following people at Inner Traditions: Vickie Trihy for your editing wizardry and integrity and Priscilla Baker and Jon Desautels for the wonderfully creative design and layout.

There are so many people who helped make this book possible. Thanks go to: Adrienne Corso, for finding me after thirty years; my Level 2 Psychic Development class for your stories and truth; the fifth graders in Mr. McDermott's class at Plain Elementary; my writer's support group; Bert Stitt; all those in my spiritual journaling classes who gave their hearts to this process; my most amazing husband and daughter; my dear friend and soul sister, Terry Haag; Shannon King for your poetry and love; Laurel Reinhardt for your wisdom; the Mostly Mondays poetry circle at the General Store, where I borrowed numerous ideas. My deepest gratitude goes to my friends Michele Belisle and Kathy Crook for their honest feedback and support. And thank you to my artistic "sisters," Geri Schrab and Arline Beagan, for their creative touch.

Throughout this book I have sprinkled gems of wisdom about writing and life from writers, poets, and other wisdomkeepers. I thank them for the insight and spirit they bring to this book and to the world, and I hope their words inspire my readers as they have inspired me.

And I thank my journals. Every time I feed them with my words and emotions, they always give something back to me.

Introduction

Morning has broken
Like the first morning,
Blackbird has spoken
Like the first bird.
Praise for the singing!
Praise for the morning!
Praise for them, springing
From the first Word.

—ELEANOR FARJEON, CHILDREN'S AUTHOR

The following story is found in many traditions. This particular version is borrowed from the Cheyenne tribe of North America.

There was a young man who was named Running Barefoot Boy because as soon as he could stand he began to run. He would run about the tribal grounds, and when he got old enough he would often run far out of sight.

Once he went running a bit too far. And soon was lost and hungry. He came upon a plum tree and, although it had been a poor season, three beautiful ripe plums hung from the tree. The branch where the plums hung was high, hanging over a deep creek. So, he took a fast run toward the tree and leapt up into the air with all his strength and grabbed at the plums. He felt the branch shake, but he quickly landed with a big splash in the creek below. As he stood up in the water, he saw the plums had fallen into the bottom of the deep moving creek. He jumped in after them but did not get them. He waited for the water to calm enough for him to see the plums and, again, in he jumped for the fruit.

Running Barefoot Boy spent three days trying to get to those juicy plums. He was hungry and determined.

Then an elder from the tribe found the boy and asked him what he was doing.

"I am going after those ripe plums that are sitting down at the bottom of the creek. I am not about to give up now, I've been at it too long."

The elder smiled and looked up at the tree.

"Young man, you are jumping in after the reflection of the plums! The real plums are still hanging in the tree branch above your head."

I wrote this book to help you, the reader, spend less time going after the illusion of what you are hungry for—and discover how to get the real thing. Fortunately, the real thing is with us all the time. It lies within us.

At the age of sixteen I began to keep a journal. I now have bookshelves full of journals. No matter what happened in my life, I had my journals to talk with, to return to, to write in, and to read. It is my journals that got me out of the creek and into the tree—where I now regularly taste the real thing.

> We are important and our lives are important, magnificent really, and their details are worthy to be recorded.
>
> —NATALIE GOLDBERG, POET, BUDDHIST TEACHER, AUTHOR OF *WRITING DOWN THE BONES*

The Internal Flame

Inside each of us is an eternal flame. This flame always burns in our soul. It is our creative flame. Our flame of purpose. Our flame of inner independence and strength. It is our connection to the creative pulse, the divine fire that is in all of life. To some it is the Tao, the unifying principle that connects and lives in all things. Buddhists refer to this inner light as our true nature. This inner fire is the essence of our divinity, our divine right. It is called by many names—Shakti, the kundalini force, the Goddess, Sri Yantra, and Bindu.

The most important thing to remember is that this internal flame is real. Real as these words on this page. Real as your heartbeat. Real as the vibration of music you hear from your favorite CD. Real as the plums in the tree. There is another story that helps illustrate this.

It is told that the indigenous peoples of the West Indies could not see Columbus and his three ships as they sat offshore. They could not see them because they had no frame of reference for such things—the ships weren't like anything they had ever witnessed before. The shaman of the tribe, however, could see ripples in the water and wavelike streams in the air where the ships sat anchored. So, he knew something was there. The shaman, knowing this, would look out each morning and gaze on the ripples in the water and in the air. He opened his mind to the possibilities of the unknown. One day, he saw what others could not—three ships sitting in the water.

"I write. The longer I live, the more convinced I've become that I cultivate my truest self in this one way."

—TOM CHIARELLA, AMERICAN WRITER

"Walk in the light of your own fire, and in the flame which ye have kindled."

—Isaiah **50:11**

He then helped his tribe's people to "see" what until then they could not see. The ships were there; they were real.

Some people in your life may not believe you have this internal flame because they cannot see it. But you can see the ripples of your flame—in your ideas, your art, your written words, your prayers, and all your creations. You may not see the wind but it pushes the branches of the tree back and forth. Every creative thought, no matter how small, how seemingly unimportant, is proof of the fire inside of you. As you keep a journal, the words and images that appear on your pages will be your ripples. And when you bring your attention to these ripples, you will end up seeing what you could not see before—your own internal flame. The ideas in this book will help remove any stuff that is piled on top of your flame, and it will allow you to be able to see your flame, and that of others, burning vividly. From this place of "sight" your life will truly be your own—you will be able to set fire to your ideas and your dreams all along the way. Your ships will suddenly appear before you. You will stop jumping into the water after an illusion and go instead for the plums in the tree. You will taste the fruit of your own creativity. And your journal will be your companion and guide.

> There is a vitality, a life force, an energy, a quickening that is translated through you into action and because there is only one of you in all time, its expression is unique. And if you block it, it will never exist through any other medium and be lost, the world will not have it.
>
> —Martha Graham, choreographer, dance teacher

Shamans, spiritual teachers, gurus, avatars, yogis, Buddhas, prophets, monks, all give us ways to touch the flame inside so we can see who we truly are, and who we can become. Just as the shaman of the tribe taught himself and others to see something they never knew existed, each of us can do the same for ourselves. Just like Running Barefoot Boy, you too can be directed to the real "plums" of life.

It can be useful to have a skillful guide to help you find or rekindle your flame—but it is the shaman inside of you that will really allow you to see and feel it for yourself. Your journals will be for you, as they were for me, spiritual companions and guides on the journey through life. They will often contain the spark that is needed to set you on fire. They will bring forth your true nature.

It all begins with fire—
Suns stars   moons Earths   me you.

This, too, commenced in flame—
This page   this ink   these words.

Books blaze blind around us—
In this room   this now   this you.

All true writing starts this way—
With you right here on fire.
        —D. W. ROZELLE, AMERICAN POET

What You Will Find in This Book

Each chapter of this book offers a series of short, simple ideas for writing that are loosely related to the chapter topic. You can start reading at the beginning and go through the book in order, or you can begin with the end and jump right on to the middle. You decide.

In every chapter there are questions you can respond to in your journal, exercises and meditations to help you get in touch with your thoughts and feelings, and "Off the Page" activities to take your journaling experiences out into your world. You'll see plenty of examples of journal writing by other young people and some of my own. In several chapters I've included longer contributions from guest writers who offer unique insights on a particular topic.

All of the topics and questions in the book are intended to spark your own ideas, so feel free to write whatever comes to you, even if

"Look at yourself through your soul's eyes. See the beauty of your being."
—**SANAYA ROMAN,**
AMERICAN AUTHOR,
PSYCHIC

it seems "off topic." Read with me and then write what you wish. But wherever you begin, pull out your journal and write.

> "Will you come with me, reader?
> I thank you. Give me your hand."
> —FROM *THE ADVENTURES OF ROBIN HOOD* BY HOWARD PYLE,
> AMERICAN ILLUSTRATOR AND STORYTELLER

The Beautiful Thing about Journaling

Being yourself is the greatest gift you can offer the world. And the time you spend with your journal will help you bring forth this gift.

The beautiful thing about journaling is that you get to work something out on the page, all to yourself, or between yourself and your spiritual source. You get to create your life on the page and see how it feels. You can work out a lot of thorny issues in your journals, which allows your life to flow more strongly and easily. If you aren't journaling already, you will see what I mean when you begin to fill the pages up with your thoughts, feelings, and ideas. Journaling can be a great lamp on your path, lighting your way.

> "The essential intent in journal writing is self-understanding. Your journal is a perfect guide: It listens without judgment and reflects who you are back to you when you read it. It is a trusted and versatile traveling companion that will be a true friend along your life's path."
> —JOHN FOX, POET AND POETRY THERAPIST,
> AUTHOR OF *FINDING WHAT YOU DIDN'T LOSE*

Your journal can also give you a sense of stability and permanence if there has been constant upheaval in your life. If you have lived in foster homes or have been separated in other ways from a parent or from your family of origin, your journals can serve as both your life storybook and a "home base."

"Advice to young writers? Always the same advice: Learn to trust your own judgment, learn inner independence, learn to trust that time will sort the good from the bad—including your own bad."

—DORIS LESSING,
NOVELIST, SHORT
STORY WRITER

Through your journal writing and time spent alone you will gain a deeper understanding of your self and hear the voice and call of your own soul. Your journal will:

- be a record of a difficult time, or a time of victory, or both.
- empower you.
- possibly become a book or part of a book.
- generate new ideas, and new perspectives on your life.
- help you to think for yourself.
- improve your ability to handle conflict.
- be a place to safely express your anger.
- show you a way to really accept yourself as you are.
- help you build a stronger connection to your spiritual source.
- become a friend to confide in.
- be a place for you to work out difficult emotions.
- make you feel more sure of yourself as you deal with your day-to-day issues.
- improve your relationships because you'll know who you are and what you want.
- be a record of your life, its events big and small.
- be a sacred place to visit and feel safe.

I have been in and out of NINE homes and I am only sixteen. When Julie recommended I keep a journal it hit me immediately as a way to record all this. To tell it like it really is. But it actually became a lot more than that—it is my sanctuary. Now, six months later, I have three entire notebooks full. Full of swear words, poetry, notes, drawings, my anger and even a bit of decent stuff. They will go with me wherever I go. It is really weird but it is important to me that I find a place to live where my journals will be safe.

—HANNAH, IN HER TENTH FOSTER HOME, WHERE SHE HAS FOUND
A SAFE PLACE FOR HERSELF AND HER JOURNALS

"Writing is always a voyage of discovery."

—NADINE GORDIMER,
SOUTH AFRICAN NOVELIST,
SHORT STORY WRITER

Introduction

Don't be too surprised if your journal entries become part of a book some day. You will find my journal writings in every one of my books. Sandra Cisneros, the young author of *The House on Mango Street,* writes of her life in a simple but powerful journal of vignettes. Anne Frank, Aldo Leopold, Anaïs Nin, and Joseph LeConte are all people whose journals were published. Of course, even if your words are used only to link yourself to yourself, this is a great act. A most wonderful act, I believe; a necessary act.

I am writing young adult fiction now. . . . Those were intense times for me, and when I began writing a strong young adult voice emerged that I've just sort of gone with. I luckily managed to hold onto journals and letters from that time in my life, which are invaluable to me now.

—ADRIENNE CORSO, NOW FORTY-SOMETHING, WHO PUBLISHED A BOOK BASED ON HER TEEN JOURNALS, ENTITLED *JUMP*

Your Living, Breathing Journal

Think of your journal as a living breathing being, someone who needs your love and attention. Don't neglect her. She loves your pen or pencil running across her pages. She loves what comes to life when you write. She feels complete with your poems and drawings. She wants more contact with you and is selfish with your time. She loves what you bring to her. Even the silly or frivolous line fills her up. She needs more food than your pet fish, and more love letters than your sweetheart.

If you give her what she needs, she rewards you. She helps you sleep at night. She is your test ground for ideas. She consumes your anger (without getting back at you). She is never insulted.

If you stay away too long, she calls to you. And when she is full of you, she sits beautifully on a shelf (or hidden in some secret spot), feeling strong and admired. She knows you will revisit her, even if it takes months or years—she knows she holds something you will want to return to.

"'What makes a desert beautiful,' said the little prince, 'is that somewhere there it hides a well.'"

—FROM *THE LITTLE PRINCE* BY ANTOINE DE SAINT-EXUPÉRY, FRENCH NOVELIST, PILOT

Can you feel her breathe? Can you hear her calling you? Go feed your journal.

* What have you gotten out of writing in a journal?
* Describe your relationship with your journal.
* When you are all finished with this book and its process, what do you hope will be different in your life? What will be the same? Write about this.

"Writing itself is one of the great, free human activities. There is scope for individuality, and elation, and discovery."

—FROM WRITING THE AUSTRALIAN CRAWL BY WILLIAM STAFFORD

1

Word Warriors

*. . . my
jaws ache for release, for
words that will say*

*anything. I force myself
to remember
who I am, what I am, and
why I am here . . .*

—PHILIP LEVINE, JEWISH AMERICAN POET

"In Japan, it is said that words of the soul reside in a spirit called kotodama or the spirit of words, and the act of speaking words has the power to change the world."

—MASARU EMOTO, JAPANESE SCIENTIST AND AUTHOR OF *THE HIDDEN MESSAGES IN WATER*

Words Are Your Power

"Sticks and stones may break my bones but names will really hurt me." This is a more honest take on the old rhyme we hear in elementary school. What people say to us and what we say to ourselves holds deep and lasting impact. In his research the Japanese scientist Masaru Emoto discovered that "water exposed to the words 'Thank you' formed beautiful geometric crystals, no matter what the language. But water exposed to 'You fool,' and other degrading words resulted in obviously broken and deformed crystals." Many healing practices and traditions throughout history use words such as *love, forgiveness,* and *thank you* to restore a person's health. Words (spoken and thought) hold powerful energy and intentions. Emoto points out that humans are made up of 70 percent water. If words can have such an effect on a glass of water, what do you think they can do to a human being?

Writing down our thoughts, ideas, and dreams gives them more power. Sometimes the power is in releasing the hold a given word has on us. Sometimes in writing our thoughts down we put together something meaningful for ourselves and for the world. The more we write and relate to our own thoughts and words, the more beautiful and strong we become.

* What you say to yourself holds an incredible amount of influence on how you feel and act. What words do you carry in your head? What words do you use to describe yourself? Write about this.
* For you, what follows the words "I am . . . "? Make a list of *I am's.*
  I am wonderful.
  I am always late.
  I am an artist.
  I am forgetful.
  I am a writer.
* Write about something you appreciate about yourself.

"Writing is the only thing that, when I do it, I don't feel I should be doing something else."

—GLORIA STEINEM, AMERICAN WRITER AND SOCIAL ACTIVIST

Word Warriors

✱ Pretend you are one of the following objects. Give one or all of these objects a voice. Write in the first person—use the words "I am . . . " Write as much as you can about this object; include any thoughts, images or impressions that come to mind.

I am a returned graduation present.

I am a romance magazine.

I am a camera.

I am . . . (choose an object in your environment).

Off the Page

Take a piece of paper and write on it positive words like *Love, Thank-you, I am wonderful*. Tape this on your water bottle for the day, or for the week. (If you don't want others to know what it says, write it in another language, or use a symbol that represents a positive word of power.)

Word Warriors: Writing as a Response

Through my journal writing I respond to my life: My friend dies of cancer; I write her a poem. My brother crashes my first car (when I was twenty-one); I write him a letter in my journal. A beautiful day is spent in the garden with my daughter; it becomes a short story. I come across my old baptismal certificate in a drawer and I write about it. . . .

I was thirteen. No one in my family had been baptized. A part of me wondered, did this mean that God would not recognize us and that we would be in hell or purgatory for eternity? I decided it would be best to get baptized. Just in case. I chose the Lutheran minister I met on one of the occasional Easter Sundays my mother took us to church. I then attended this church on my own between the ages of ten and fourteen.

I remember one of my favorite sermons: A man was on a cliff. Below him was a drop to his death and above a hungry tiger. He hung there for some time. The tiger would not move, and there was no other way to go but up to the tiger or down to his death. Next to him, a delicious ripe strawberry grew. He reached to eat the strawberry and fell to his death.

I, too, was reaching for something beautiful, something real.

The day the minister baptized me, he spoke to me of what it might mean to be baptized. I felt safer somehow; if this was the ticket into the after-life, now I had it. He walked into the other room to get a bowl of water. "Holy water," I thought. He came out saying, "It's just tap water, Julie." He was try-ing to teach me the bigger lesson here: you don't need this to get into heaven, to be close to God, or to know the truth. He graciously baptized me with the tap water and I left that day with my baptismal certificate.

Baptized by tap water. Something about that small, personal ritual worked for me. The minister himself went on to another calling, and I went on to learn about the Quakers' approach to God, and then I moved on to Bud-dhism and meditation. Today when I hear a spiritual teacher claim that he, and he alone, holds the key to the kingdom, I remember my baptism.

"It's just tap water." But tap water and Jesus, and the Buddha and I, and you, we all come from the same sacred source.

And for this reason something good sticks.

* Go open a drawer or box in your room. Write a response to some-thing you find in there.
* For at least a week make writing your *first* response to whatever comes into your life.

It is such a surprise to me to write first and then do something. I would have quit a class for sure if I hadn't written a letter to the teacher in my journal first. I got all the tears and sweat on the paper and somehow found the means to finish the class.

—NERITA, AGE 21

Word Warriors

Word Warriors

14

> Journal writing is awesome. I can say anything to anybody without hurting them. And without pissing them off. . . . I broke up with my girlfriend of eight months last week and I wish I had written in my journal first. I regret what I did. It can be hard to have writing be the first response—but I bet it will save my butt many times.
>
> —Bird, age 15, who plans on using his journals to write a science-fiction novel

* Experiencing a difficulty? Write about it first, and then do something about it.
* Write about an experience that each of these words recalls. Try about five minutes on each: *embarrassed; secrets; afraid; borrowed; Jesus; road trip.*

Pointers to the Truth

> "The man pulling radishes
> pointed the way
> with a radish."
>
> —Issa, Japanese haiku poet (1763–1827)

So many times my young students and readers say, "I don't know what to believe." They want to know and live The Truth. I invite them to consider all the spiritual and religious teachings, and even all the self-help books, as pointers, arrows that can point to the truth. Pointers to the truth but not, in and of themselves, The Truth. Even the most sacred of texts and the wisdom contained within them can be understood as "pointers" to truth. When we approach spiritual teachings (whatever tradition they come from) as pointers, we can step into a more real experience with spiritual truth that is inherent in all the world's religious practices.

How? By realizing that words on paper, or someone else's interpretation of something sacred, cannot in themselves be The Truth.

They are pointing to something, saying, Hey, look—this is the color, the shape, and the texture of this beautiful thing. Now see if you can go find it for yourself. When all the words in the Bible or the Koran or the Bhagavad-Gita are understood as pointers, then each of us can search for the meaning they contain for ourselves. When we use a guidebook on birds, we know the pictures and words are not the actual bird but pointers to what to look for. In the same way, we can look at what a sacred text is directing us toward and go experience the truth for ourselves.

No one owns the truth. Fortunately, it comes in many flavors and designs. We each get to understand and experience truth (and various spiritual teachings) in our own way.

I do not consider myself as "spiritual." I don't really believe in a god or a bigger power. I believe in nature and like to read naturalists like James G. Cowen, Wendell Berry, Aldo Leopold, and John Muir. And they all point to the same thing, that we are just a part of a big web. We are not the center. It points to the truth that we are part of something natural and it is natural law that we must listen to.

—Ben, age 21

The bible (the new testament) points to love and forgiveness.

—Tammie, age 14

✦

✱ Consider the religious or humanitarian teachings you have encountered in your life. What are they pointing to? Write about this.

This is a story of a young woman who had great faith. A flood hit her town with such severity that all the people were washed away or had only a few hours to save themselves and their belongings. The water quickly reached the stairs leading to this woman's house. As she sat praying on her porch, some

"I started to discover I was being more honest when I was inventing, more truthful when dreaming."

—Michael Ondaatje, Sri Lankan novelist, poet, screenwriter

friends came by in a boat and said, "Come on with us, or you'll drown!" But the woman of faith said no, and rejected her friends' invitation. "Thank you, but God will surely save me."

Another hour passed and the young woman prayed and prayed, believing in her heart that God would surely save her. The water had now reached her roof and a boat full of neighbors came by. "The boat is crowded but we have room for you. Come on!" "No," the young woman replied, "God will save me."

Not too much later she was on her chimney, still praying, still having faith that God would save her. All that could be seen for miles and miles was green rushing water and a few other chimneys. As she sat there praying in earnest, another boat came by with a stranger in it. "Young lady," the stranger called, "come in my boat and save yourself!" But again, she resisted and said, "God will save me."

It was but moments later that this young woman found herself in the presence of God. Angrily she said to God, " I prayed and prayed for you to save me. I believed in you. I have done good my entire life, and you let me drown!"

And God gently said, "My daughter, I sent you three boats and you rejected them all."

* What are you praying for these days? What are the "boats" life is sending you?
* What does it mean to "be careful what you pray for"?
* Write about a sign from God.

In Other Words . . .

In school we are often encouraged to let others think for us; we are told how to think and what to think. We are given someone's ideas of what happened (in our history books) and we are told to take it as fact. Often others confuse their personal interpretation of history as facts. Writers of history books hold a lot of power—educating the minds of millions of Americans. Historians invent history, in many ways. They are given some facts and then they fill in a lot of blanks with their interpretation of the facts. For hundreds of years only white men wrote our history books. How might this influence what goes into these textbooks?

And it is not just in history class that we may find facts and truth being confused. This can even happen in art class or creative writing classes. We are told that the opposite of white is black. We are told where to put commas and how to paint a tree.

The way we open up to our truth is by listening to ourselves, and by creating new ideas for ourselves. We open up to our truth by interpreting history, and other lessons, for ourselves. How many of us believe that the opposite of soft is hard? The opposite of black is white? The opposite of up is down? How many of us believe that Columbus discovered America? Do you think Native American history claims that Columbus discovered America? How many know the presidents of the United States but none of the great North American Indian Chiefs?

One of the beautiful things about writing is that we can invent new ideas, meanings, even places that no one has ever traveled to. We can take a look at something from an entirely new perspective. I wonder what the turkey's take on the Thanksgiving feast would be?

* Invent some opposites. Try to stretch your imagination and not invent an obvious opposite, but something unique, maybe even silly or odd.

  What is the opposite of blue jeans?
  What is the opposite of a Saturday?
  What is the opposite of an airport?
  What is the opposite of green?

* Now take these opposites and write a poem or a short vignette with them. Let your self imagine and invent. Don't go to the obvious place.

Word Warriors

The opposite of blue jeans is a hard cover book; the opposite of a Saturday is detention hall; the opposite of an airport is an inch worm; the opposite of green is lazy.

The blue jeans sat on my legs like a hard cover book that has never been opened
there is so much of me
that has never been opened.
I sit green and lazy with my mind moving like an airport.
I am sitting in detention hall, again, the clock moving like an inchworm.
All I know is I want it to be Saturday.

—Crystal, age 17

✱ Now, what is the opposite of you?

The opposite of me is pink.

—Allie, age 15, who prefers baggy black clothes

The opposite of me is a gambling hall and a deck of cards. The opposite of me is a martini on the rocks and a lonely boring Sunday. The opposite of me is early morning news on TV and a dune buggy. The opposite of me is a blank look, high skinny heels on shoes, good hair days; flat tummies and a blank movie screen. The opposite of me is the shallow end of the pool and sitting quietly in the back row of the room.

—Author's journal, 2005

Off the Page

It's likely you have stumbled across a lesson in a class that just doesn't feel right to you. Trust that feeling and go find another way of looking at that particular time in history—or that particular way to write a paragraph. Or find something that is not factually true in your history book. Write up a report on it and hand it in for extra credit.

Re-Thinking TV

Writing this book has had some lasting impact on me. I know how important it is to live what you teach. Okay, I may not follow through on every lesson, all the time. But I do practice the principles I teach. . . .

So, the other night I was watching *Law and Order.* It was late and I had already seen this show. Where we live we receive channels only if we are hooked up to a satellite provider. The satellite provider was showing advertisements at the time asking the viewer to "Re-Think TV." One ad had a child moving through a house, and every time he entered a room, where the pivotal piece of furniture was a television, he would be ten years older. Central to this person's life was TV. As an additional promotion this satellite provider gave an hour of free service to anyone who got someone else to subscribe. So, my husband and I rethought TV. A few days later, I called the satellite TV company and let them know that we did indeed rethink TV—and had decided to cancel our satellite subscription.

It felt wonderful—powerful. A little blank at times—looking for what else to do to relax or pass the evening. I don't think (ha ha!) that this is what they had in mind. Now my evenings include reading out loud to my daughter, watching the sunset, reading another great book, watching a movie (DVD) without commercials, and, of course, writing in my journal.

❖

Rethink TV.

* How are individuals of your age and background depicted on TV?
* Your TV is broken, and cannot be repaired or replaced anytime soon.
* My father watched TV all day and all night the year he was dying. It was company for him. The day after he died the television went on by itself. Write about how this happened.
* Watch the sunset and write about it.

"TV is sometimes accused of encouraging fantasies. Its real problem, though, is that it encourages— enforces, almost—a brute realism. It is anti-Utopian in the extreme. We're discouraged from thinking that, except for a few new products, there might be a better way of doing things."

—BILL MCKIBBEN,
NATURALIST, AUTHOR OF
THE END OF NATURE

Word Warriors

✱ Make a list of fifty things you can do besides watch TV. What are you waiting for?

Re-Write . . . Your Life

Rewriting is one of my favorite aspects of the writer's life. Really! I get to stretch, change, add, and take away from something already written. Here too the writer's life mirrors my spiritual life. I can also rewrite my life. And you too can rewrite whatever you have already written or created.

You get to rewrite a poem, an idea, a relationship, even a plan that you have already begun to carry out; you too can rewrite your life. It is a big distortion to say that once you make a decision, make a promise, get it down on paper, or have it quoted in an interview you can never, ever change your mind. Or that changing your mind is a sign of weakness and lack of commitment. It is actually a sure sign of self-esteem and personal power. You can change your mind; you can return to something that you have already done and do it over again. In fact at certain times of our lives, our young adult years being one of them, we need to be able to change our minds, rewrite what has already been written, and begin again.

If the worst thing someone can say about me is that I change my mind (a lot) then hurray for me. I've come to realize that my mind is one thing I have the right to change as often as I like. This means I get to reconsider my choices, try them on for size and see if they really work for me. I can say yes to something and then realize that, no, this is not for me. And fortunately, I get to rewrite my written words. I cannot think of a book, an article, or even a letter of mine that didn't involve some rewriting.

How often do we change our minds about relationships? Clothing? Plans? Meals? How about what college to attend, or whether or not to go to college at all? Where to travel and what to do once we get there? I think you get the idea. Changing your mind/rewriting your life is a good skill to have on the path of life, and a necessary skill to have in writing and any creative process.

The great thing about writing is—we can rewrite our histories and our stories!

* Choose an uncomfortable or painful time in the recent or distant past. Take a few moments to remember what it was about this experience that was painful for you. Take some nice deep breaths as you remember and maybe even feel the pain of the time.

    Now rewrite it. Let something different happen. Begin it as it happened and then add some things and take some things away. How would you have liked it to proceed? What would you choose to leave out, or add?
* Rewrite a relationship.
* Bring to mind a happy ending. Now rewrite it.
* Look at one of your poems, journal entries, or short stories and add to it:

    a strange crowd
    a favorite dessert
    an unopened birthday gift
    dirty hands

Notice how the piece changes as you weave in these themes.

Off the Page

Now take your life—where you are at, right now—and add these themes to it:

    a morning sunrise
    ending a bad thing
    consulting an oracle (see Chapter 3)
    a hopeful thought

Notice how your life changes as you bring these themes into it.

"Sometimes I feel like a figment of my own imagination."

—A CHARACTER IN A COMEDY SKETCH BY JANE WAGNER

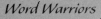

2

Finding Your Song: Poetic Medicine

Butterflies in the Mud

I carry a sprig of insanity
Deep in my bouquet of life
As I walk down the aisle
The world claims me as its wife
But tonight my headache's lifted
As I settle into sleep
I free the butterflies from the mud
And one is mine to keep.

—LIA JOY RUNDLE, POET, ARTIST

Soul Song: An African Tradition

In some African tribes, when a woman becomes pregnant she goes out into the wilderness with some other women. Together they meditate and pray until they all hear the song that belongs to that new child. They know that every soul has its own sound and vibration. This song helps everyone know this child and his or her purpose in life.

The women then return to the tribe and teach this child's song to everyone. No child's song is like any other.

When the child is born, everyone gathers and sings the song. Then when the child begins to go to school, the village gathers again and chants the child's song. They sing it again together when each child passes into the initiation of adulthood, and when he or she marries.

Finally, when the soul is passing from this world to the next, the family and friends gather around and sing that person's unique song, as they did at birth, singing the soul into the next life.

In these African tribes there is one other occasion when all the people will gather and sing someone their song—if this person has committed any crime or harmful social act. The individual is asked to stand in the middle of the circle and the entire village chants the song.

This is done because when one recognizes one's own true song, a person has no desire or need to do anything that would hurt others. The song brings the offenders back to themselves, to their community and the love that connects them all.

You may not have grown up in an African tribe that chants your soul's song to you. But there is a song for you nevertheless. You may have heard your song in your dreams; you may have sung it yourself, or heard it moving through the air when you were outside in natural surroundings. . . .

Every soul has a song.

"A poet friend of mine told me that his poems know far more than he does, and if he listens to them, they teach him."

—FROM *A RING OF ENDLESS LIGHT* BY MADELEINE L'ENGLE, AUTHOR OF YOUNG ADULT FICTION

Finding Your Song

The Soul Knows

I am a singer. I have always been a singer. My soul speaks to me through song. I feel connected to Spirit while using my voice. My first performance was at our family church.

At age twelve, I was practicing a hymn with one of the pastors. While going through the hymn, I felt and heard an embellishment and used my voice to share this idea. Pastor R. stopped me. He said "Oh, no. You can't do that. You can't sing like that. That's not how the song goes. You have to stay on one note and not move your voice around." When I asked why, his reply was "Because Jesus is the same yesterday, today, and tomorrow." This was his reason? I was confused. I felt like I did something wrong. So, I sang it the way he told me was right.

But the soul knows. The soul knows no rules. This man could not stifle my song. Luckily, I listened to Spirit. Today, I sing what I feel. My songs are full of soul.

—SHAWNI MARKS, YOUNG ADULT SINGER-SONGWRITER

Shawni wrote the following lyrics after the suicide of her father. You can hear this song by going to my Web site: julietallardjohnson. com.

REMNANTS OF CRAZY

Remnants of crazy only remain
You left me here
While you left insane
What feels like pity
Is anger the same
It's hard to pick up the pieces
Without placing the blame

You gotta gotta
Keep movin' Keep movin'
You gotta gotta
Keep movin' Keep movin'

And then I will heal

There are no rules
In this game of grief
Can't borrow no money
To buy some relief
Searching for mercy
Asking for grace
Why didn't you answer?
Before the mistake?

You gotta gotta
Keep movin' keep movin'
You gotta gotta
Keep movin' keep movin'
And then I will heal.

You gotta keep movin'
Moving through
Moving on
Moving up

Sometimes you don't win
Sometimes you just finish

And that is enough

Keep moving
Keep going
Keep driving

To keep thriving

Keep moving

Keep running
Keep giving

To stay living

Gotta gotta keep movin' . . .

* Everyone has a song; write yours.
* Who tried to stifle your voice?
* Write about a time someone made you feel that you'd done something wrong, but you knew you hadn't.
* Work with "Remnants of Crazy" to change the words around and write your own poem.

Off the Page

Set one of your poems to music.

Poetic Medicine

If you can just get the pen to paper, you might not hurt so much. You might get all the pain—or enough of it, anyway—on paper and feel better, freer. Writing poetry is good medicine. By the age of sixteen, Lia had developed the destructive habit of cutting herself when she was sad or upset. That year she decided to write instead of continuing to cut herself. She put together a powerful collection of poems that she published in a chapbook, *Butterflies in the Mud.* * Here is what she says about her poem, which appears below: "This is a very

---

*Lia's poetry book can be purchased at julietallardjohnson.com. All proceeds go to Lia.

"In its origin a poem is something completely unequivocal. It is a discharge, a call, a cry, a sigh, a gesture, a reaction by which the living soul seeks to defend itself from or to become aware of an emotion, an experience. In this first spontaneous most important function no poem can be judged. It speaks first of all simply to the poet himself, it is his cry, his scream, his dream, his smile, his whirling fists."

—HERMANN HESSE, GERMAN NOVELIST

private poem, and one I hesitate to include in this compilation. I know some of you will understand this immediately and know why it makes me feel so exposed. This is another poem referring to the self-injury—deep emotions played out in shallow wounds. . . . My comfort 'lies' in every meaning of the words, *beneath my sweater*."

Instead of harming herself, Lia wrote in her journal and filled pages with her poetry.

BENEATH MY SWEATER
Beneath my sweater
my theme song's playing
Beneath my sweater
I feel the burn
Beneath my sweater
I didn't even cry
Beneath my sweater
I finish what I've started
Beneath my sweater
I crucify my savior/myself
Beneath my sweater
my left hand's stronger than my right
Beneath my sweater
I'm the only one who knows
Beneath my sweater
my scars shine through
Beneath my sweater
my death is revived
Beneath my sweater
my comfort lies
Beneath my sweater
I fall into myself
Beneath my sweater
I call it me
Beneath my sweater . . .

✱ Using a repeating phrase (as Lia did in "Beneath My Sweater") write a poem. Here are some possible phrases you can repeat:

    She always told me . . .

    Away from here . . .

    If they only knew . . .

    Each day the sun calls . . .

✱ Write a poem about what hurts.

✱ Write a poem using the following words:

    runaway

    trapped inside

    a sacred place

    a double rainbow

    another sin

    somehow released

✱ Every poem has a story. Next to any poem you have written, write the story behind it, its meaning, as Lia did above.

Poetic Vision

We tend to write about and acknowledge what we know, and ignore what we don't notice or what we forget. Research shows that we tend to order the same food at our favorite restaurant; we tend to always notice the same objects in a room that we frequent—we tend to choose the familiar over the new, and most people are afraid of change. But with the heart and eyes of a poet, even our favorite food tastes different; every room can be new; and change is just another source of poetry.

Poetry can be our guide, our lamp through difficult times, but it can also allow us to see beyond the ordinary and beyond our habitual way of seeing and experiencing the world. In trying to write a poem for my daughter's second grade teacher, I find myself looking into the classroom for prompts, for ideas. Because of this I see more—and

I find what I want to write about. When I look with the eyes of a poet I always discover something I would have otherwise missed.

* Write about what you don't remember. Repeat the phrase, *I don't remember* instead of stopping your hand. Try to fill up a page.

  I don't remember the name of my third grade teacher; I don't remember what I wanted to be when I grew up; I don't remember my first kiss; I don't remember my father ever reading to me; I don't remember anything before the age of eight; I don't remember . . ."

  Write more on any of these.

* Now write a poem using all or some of the above.

* Sit outside for fifteen minutes and listen to the sounds of nature. Write about the sounds you hear. Just listen and write. After this, write about what you don't remember . . . using the sounds you just recorded, as Marybeth did in the poem below.

> *It was the momentum of a time capsule life,*
> *closed and sleeping,*
> *my ears were plugged,*
> *my eyes were covered, and*
> *my Soul was contained.*
>
> *I don't remember hearing*
> *the meadow larks,*
> *the mourning doves, or*
> *the silent growing of grass.*
>
> *That was then,*
> *This is now.*
> *I have time to listen to the larks,*
> *the doves,*
> *and if I really listen,*
> *I can hear the grass grow.*
>
> **—MARYBETH BERG, WRITER, POET, ARTIST, PRIESTESS**

Finding Your Song

* Take a fresh look at a family member and write about him or her from a poet's perspective. Find at least five characteristics or features you have overlooked in this person.
* Write a poem about your bedroom, looking for images you are so used to that you normally overlook them.

Off the Page

Order something new from a restaurant menu and write about it.

Poetic Questions

Oftentimes your poems can come from questions you hold inside. Why did this happen to me? When will I feel better? How can I be so lucky? Who are my true friends? What happens next? What is all this about? Who is he to me anyway? How do I feel around this person? Why do I want to be her friend? Our questions, both the small and the big ones, are quite poetic. When we become aware of the questions we carry in our hearts, we become more aware of why we are feeling the way we do, and what we can do about it.

Most of us spend too much time trying to answer the question rather than listening to the question. When we get good at listening to the question we find the answers come naturally. Often, the answer is in the question itself.

Poetry helps us listen to the questions.

* Write a list of questions (big and small). Make a poem from these. Add other sentences, if you want. Christine Lee, age 17, chose these questions:

Why does he call me bitch?
Where are we going after this?
Why did my parents name me Christine Lee?
Who left me that note on my locker?
Who are my real friends?
Where are we going from here?
What am I going to do with my summer?

Here's Christine's poem:

He calls me bitch
and purses his lips.

where are we going after this
where are we going after this?

My parents name me Christine Lee
without ever meeting me

where are we going from here
where are we going from here?

Anonymous love notes
just who are my friends?

where are we going from here
where are we going from here?

The last summer approaches
like last night's dream I forgot to record.

where are we going from here?
where are we going from here?

After writing this poem Christine noticed how worried she had been feeling about her future.

Knowing how worried I was helped me calm down some. I realize that my life has a way of working out—and stressing out isn't helping me. Where am I going from here? I am going to hang out this summer and work at a local restaurant for some cash. And I am pretty sure where I am going after high school.

Meet Raven Hail

Firelight
Is the flame of the Fire eternal—
or does it burn just for tonight?
One way or another
the heart of the matter
is spirit and Shadow and Light!

—RAVEN HAIL, CHEROKEE ELDER, WRITER, POET

Today, I woke up to a pile of cow dung sitting in the middle of my path! Now, I wasn't happy about this. Of course, my mind began searching for the reasons for this—why do I feel this way, and who is responsible for this pile of dung on my path? Fortunately I remembered to consult the I Ching and it offered (as usual) great advice. So I went downstairs to write (this book that you hold in your hands).

I needed a lead poem or story for a chapter. As I pulled out one book after another, one fell out: *Ravensong: Cherokee Indian Poetry* by Raven Hail. So I began to read it, and the poems leapt off the page and filled my heart and mind with good things. The pile of cow dung evaporated. I looked to the front of the book where I found the author's name, address, and phone number. Normally I would jot it down with the intention of writing her for permission to use some of her poems. Instead, some still voice inside of me told me to dial her number. So I did. After a few short rings, she answered the phone.

Raven Hail was kind and generous enough to give me an hour of her time. More words of hers filled my mind and heart with good things. Sadly, she died just months after we spoke.

As a Cherokee she had been collecting stories, songs, poetry, wisdom, history, and relics of the Cherokee nation all her adult life, so that after she died, her people's history could live. When I read her poems I knew—this was a person who had lived through the dark night and seen the rising sun, many times. This was someone whose poems tell you secrets only your heart can understand. This was someone who used her poetry to heal and grow. Here is my favorite.

Ghigua's Song (Gaia, The Goddess)

I sang in the morning
In the rising sun,
In the rippling rhythm
Where the waters run
To the redbird promise
of eternal spring
In love and life and everything.

Sing! Sing! The circle goes around;
The fire in the center is My sacred mound.
The Smoke is a covenant between you and Me;
For I am The Singer of The Song, said She.

I sang in the middle
Of the blazing noon
With the sweat and the tears
Of a lonesome tune
Through the long hard struggle
When hope was gone;
But I am The Song and The Song lives on!

"We must learn to see the world anew."

—**Albert Einstein,**
theoretical physicist

Finding
Your Song

I danced in the evening
When the moon was thin
To the drumming rhythm
of the Thunder Men.
I danced in the lightning
And touched the earth,
A spark of light that brought rebirth.

Dance! Dance! The circle goes around;
The Fire in the center is My sacred mound.
The Smoke is a covenant between you and Me;
For I am The Lady of The Dance, said She.

I danced in the middle
Of the darkest night
In the blackness covering
Wrong from right.
They buried My name
and thought I was gone;
But I am the Dance and The Dance Lives on!

✱ What would you like to begin collecting, so that it can live on?

✱ Read Raven's poem again. Can you borrow from her flow and emotion and write one like it, as I did below?

> I shouted at the sky
> In the star lit night,
> In the fiery darkness
> Where the body hides
> its secret stories
> of the winged ones
> In faith and hope and ceremony.

Off the Page

What poetry books are falling off your shelf? Go read some and be inspired.

Write, e-mail, or make a phone call to a favorite poet, if he or she is alive. You can find out more about Raven Hail by Googling her name or by visiting my Web site: julietallardjohnson.com

Symbolic Sight: The Power of Metaphors

> Shout!
> Whisper . . .
> Beat the drum!
> Make the mountains
> sing!
>
> —RAVEN HAIL

Metaphor is the language of the soul—it is how the soul perceives the world. Metaphor connects two unlike things to create an image that is both surprising and instantly understood. Literally speaking, we know someone doesn't have a frog in his or her throat, yet we understand that language at a level that is beyond words. Searching for metaphor is using your symbolic sight and helps you open up to a more soulful perception of the world.

> "Perceiving similarity of shape in dissimilar things is certainly not logical, but it strikes us as ingenious—and that is the power of metaphor: to surprise us, make us catch our breath, illumine an aspect of the world that is totally at odds with the conventional way of seeing it."
>
> —GABRIELE LUSSER RICO, *WRITING THE NATURAL WAY*

Metaphor anchors us to all that is around us and all that is within

"Hey, look. There is God's nose!"

—AUTHOR'S 8-YEAR-OLD DAUGHTER, LYDIA ISHMAEL, POINTING TO A HILL

Finding Your Song

us. Metaphors require that we open our minds to imagine a similarity in dissimilar objects. This open-mindedness helps us in our desire to become more independent while remaining anchored to all that we value in our life. We are always changing; we are becoming independent yet increasingly aware of how we are kindred with all living things. The spiritual journey of independence is a living metaphor—we experience our inner independence as we increase our connection to all of life.

When we have the ability to perceive the similar in what is dissimilar we can see with the eyes of the soul.

What are the stars? The table scraps of the ancestors.

What is your nose? A landing strip for a bug.

What is the moon? It's a portal.

✳ Answer these questions with a metaphoric response. . . . Let your mind and soul play (there are no rules):

What was my latest phone conversation?

What is the moon?

What is the first evening star?

What are the contents of your refrigerator?

What is your craving for potato chips?

What is today?

|| Today is a hand print in moving water.—TAMARA, AGE 17

✳ Now, write a poem using your metaphors.
✳ Describe yourself through qualities you have in common with nature or animals:

My skin is a painted horse.

My hair is . . .

My legs are . . .

My elbows are . . .

My chest is . . .

My thighs are . . .

My eyebrows are . . .

Choose any part or all of your body for this exercise.

✸ Using metaphors, describe an experience you are having right now in your life.

Similes also bring different and unlike things together using the words "like" or "as." In simile, one thing is compared to another while in metaphor one thing is said to be the other. For me, a simile helps me see beyond the obvious, where nothing is just as it appears. What I see becomes more than it actually is—a phone call from a friend is like a soft rain on rock. The evening sunset is like a report card from God. You get the idea.

✦

So, when you need some surprises in your life, create a simile. Creating a simile is like crossing a bridge between a "yes" and a "no."

✸ Complete these sentences using similes:

The girl's hair was as snarled as . . .

The girl's hair was as snarled as a kite caught in the apple tree.

His voice cracked like . . .

His voice cracked like warm water hitting an ice cube.

Her blue jeans hung on her like . . .

The night-light was like . . .

Hearing gospel music is like . . .

My poetry is as . . .

✸ What are some similes you might use in describing your parents, for example?

My mom is as (cheerful, tough, light) as . . .

My dad is as (nervous, goofy, thick) as . . .

✸ Take five things from your immediate environment and create similes with them.

✸ Bored in class? Keep a notebook handy and think up new metaphors and similes. See the world symbolically.

"Listening to a liar is like drinking warm water."

—**Native American**
wisdom

Finding
Your Song

Meet Issa

Issa is the pen name for the Japanese haiku poet Issa Kobayashi. He was born in 1763 and died in 1827. At the age of three he lost his mother and was later mistreated by his stepmother. He once wrote that he never went to bed without crying in his younger years. He lived a very impoverished life, absent of peace and family love. Later in his life, he lost his wife in childbirth and four of his children died in infancy. Marriage to his second wife was unhappy. Yet, he was known for his kind and simple nature. He loved animals and often spoke up for those in need.

How is it he triumphed over these horrific losses? Where did he get this reserve of compassion and strength? Is it possible that seeing the world through a poet's eyes helped him? Did his ability to see all the metaphors alive around him make him strong?

During his lifetime Issa wrote over twenty thousand haiku poems. He also kept journals. A very popular one was his poetic diary entitled *Oraga ga Haru* (The Year of My Life), published in 1819. In it he records his life and his spiritual path, memories, and the cycles of nature. "But this poor tree has neither the strength to put forth fruits and flowers, nor the good fortune quite to die. Existence is a continuous struggle to simply put one foot high." Here are a few of his haiku poems:

> Come with me and play
> Parentless sparrow.

> The snow is melting
> and the village is flooded
> with children.

> All the time I pray to Buddha
> I keep on
> Killing mosquitoes.

Quiet
in the depths of the lake
A peak of cloud.

Haiku poetry is intentionally simple, traditionally a three-line poem with lines consisting of five, seven, and five syllables. Words are plain but the haiku uses symbolism and metaphor to bring you into the moment the poet is writing about. Haiku is like a photograph that captures the essence of what the poet is experiencing. The power of haiku comes from the way it describes natural situations in the fewest possible words, using images of nature.

writing this verse now
as the spring storm stirs outside
head full of thunder.

—**Julie Tallard Johnson**

* Write a haiku poem.
* Write about someone's life you admire.
* Write about true courage.
* Look around you right now; write a haiku poem about where you are, using an image from nature as a way to describe your experience.

Off the Page

Share your poetry on my blog at julietallardjohnson.com.

3

Dreams and Oracles: The Language of Spirit

Let us see, is this real,
Let us see, is this real,
This life I am living?
You, Spirits, you dwell everywhere,
Let us see, is this real,
This life I am living?

—PAWNEE SONG

"Dreams are . . . illustrations from the book
your soul is writing about you."
—MARSHA NORMAN, AMERICAN PLAYWRIGHT

Becoming Whole, by Geri Schrab, inspired by Wisconsin petroglyph site

"How will you dream
if you do not sleep?
How will you hear
yourself?"
—FROM *MORNING GIRL*
BY MICHAEL DORRIS

Journaling Your Dreams

Again I found myself dreaming about him. Even waking up in the morning with the feel and scent of him on my skin. It was disturbing! I had been having these dreams for over ten years—yet the last I had seen of him (in the flesh) was when we were saying good-bye, both heading off to graduate school. In this latest dream, like all the others, we were trying to reunite but something or someone kept getting in our way. I lay in my bed for a while and wondered, What do I need to do about these dreams? I want them to stop. I feel lonely waking in the morning, alone, having just dreamt of my college sweetheart. I decided to call a friend who would help me put together a personal ritual that would allow me to release him once and for all. . . . I did not expect what happened next in my life but I should have thought of the possibility. . . .

—AUTHOR'S JOURNAL, 1994

"Sometimes dreams are wiser than waking."

—BLACK ELK, SIOUX

MEDICINE MAN

I first met Bill when I was thirteen and he was fourteen. He remembers my blue eyes (caked in black eyeliner and blue eye shadow). I remember he was a drummer in a band. We dated for three months. We broke up over my flirting with a new boy in school. (See Why Girls Go for Bad Boys on pages 181–83. Bill would not speak to me. I was devastated. I walked the distance home alone, crying and angry with myself. I went to my mother who gave me a piece of wisdom: "If it is meant to be, you will be together again." Somehow this felt true to me. We went through middle school and high school without our paths crossing again.

After high school, I attended a small private college, only to return home a year later to attend the nearby university. I was pining over another lost relationship and wasn't much interested in going out. But a friend talked me into going to an outdoor concert. There, with his hair pulled back in a ponytail, was Bill. We were immediately drawn to each other and ended up going out for the next four years as we both attended the university. We ended our relationship when we went off to different graduate schools. We had some contact for the first six months, but soon our paths completely divided from each another.

I moved to Minneapolis and began to have my Bill dreams, which I recorded each time in my journal. In each dream we were trying to get together, or get married, and something prevented our reunion. After about ten years of dreaming sporadically about Bill, my dreams of him began to increase. This bothered me. I didn't contact him because I knew he was married and I didn't want to cause either one of us unnecessary pain. At the time my journals were

Dreams and Oracles

my most intimate companion. I poured my responses to my dreams into them. Not only did I record the dreams, but I wrote letters to Bill (unsent, of course). Finally, I called my friend and we performed a ritual in which I burned all his pictures and his letters to me. In the ritual I asked that the dreams stop, and that if he needed to get in contact with me he would do so.

The dreams continued. This was the year my father died. I returned home for the wake, which was held at my parents' house. I dreamed of Bill the night before. And late into the day of my father's wake, Bill showed up. I was drawn to him and felt an overpowering sense that he was my soul mate. Only, I thought he was still married (we didn't talk about those things that day). We said good-bye to each other once again. It took me five months to write him a thank-you note.

Then I dreamed we got married.

I was very happy about this because I understood that Bill represented the "male" part of me, and that this dream wedding meant my male and female energies were united within me.

I came home one day to find a bulky envelope in the mailbox for me. It was from Bill. It was full of pictures. At first I didn't want to read the letter or look at the pictures—of his happy life without me. But as I read on, he told me that he was no longer married.

We soon reunited. Together we read over all my Bill dreams, which were contained safely in my journals. We are now living "happily ever after" in Wisconsin with our daughter. We have been together now ten years.

Listen to your dreams. Record your dreams in your journal. The dream world is a very big, powerful, soulful world. Dreams are like letters, and when you write them down and read them the letters are then opened and the message received. And who do you suppose is the sender of your dreams? Many spiritual traditions tell us that some dreams are from the Creator—from the spirit world. Often the messages are from our very own souls, offering us guidance and hope.

"Earth, ourselves, breathe and awaken, leaves are stirring, all things moving, new day coming, life renewing."

—PAWNEE PRAYER

Dreams and Oracles

I dreamt I was married to my mom. Twice young men were interested in me and then they found out I was married to my mother. They weren't objecting to her being my mother as much as the age difference. She was lying on the sofa. Two men came into the room. One whispered, "Is she married?" Pointing at me. The other one said, "Yes, to her," pointing to my mother.

I then got up and went into my bedroom and looked into the mirror. I told myself I couldn't stay married to my mother. I thought that if I knew someone who was married to their mom it would be strange. I decided to tell my mom I wanted a divorce. I went out and she was sitting at a table with a glass and some wine in a bottle. She had a sense of what I was going to tell her. She poured the wine into the glass and it spilled over. I told her it would be better if she didn't drink. I also told her that I was not going to drink with her anymore. Then I walked out of her house on my own.

In my day life, I did stop drinking with her. As a result my relationship with her changed dramatically. These dreams guided me to protect myself when it came to my mother. They helped me become whole. They were personal dreams that held a message, a vision for me. I believe we all have such dreams, such messages that are attempting to help us and guide us.

—ANNETTE, AGE 23

✦

✱ Begin by writing last night's dream or your most recent dream. You can draw it if that feels like the best way to record what you remember. If you can't recall a recent dream, journal about any dream you may remember. I write my dreams in my journal, while some people have special journals just for dreams. It is best to write the dreams as soon as you can, as soon as you wake up, if possible, before you forget them.

Off the Page

Tibetan Dream Yoga

Tibetans practice an elaborate (but not difficult) process of dream yoga that allows people to use their dreams to become more present and happy in life. It is an ancient process that can teach you to "awaken" in your dreams and receive the visions that appear in your dream time. You can tune in more clearly to the visions in your dreams by following the suggestions below, which are based on the Tibetan model:

- Record your dreams in your journal. This can be done by drawing your dreams or by writing them out.
- Listen to your dreams and respond to them, as Annette did in the example on page 44. She let her dreams play an important role in guiding her decisions, and ultimately the course of her life. Consider your dreams letters or messages from your true nature or the spirit world. What is being communicated to you?
- Before you go to sleep at night, ask for some guidance in your dream. Then to help with remembering dreams, traditional Tibetan practice instructs boys to lie on their right side and girls, on their left.
- Share your dreams with trusted friends, your therapist, or your spiritual adviser.
- Notice what images, feelings, sensations, experiences, and encounters you had in your night dreams also occur in the daytime.
- Read a good book on dreams for teens, such as *Teen Dream Power* by M. J. Abadie.

"All situations can be used to deepen our understanding and the sense of magic and beauty in our experience."

—JACK KORNFIELD, BUDDHIST TEACHER AND PSYCHOLOGIST

Nightmares

> "Every nightmare hints at the secret reserves of imaginative
> power in the human mind."
>
> —John Gardner, American novelist

No matter what form your dreams take, know that they always contain a message of hope. The same can be said about consulting an oracle (see pages 59–61): if the message of the oracle is not one of hope then either you are interpreting it wrong, or the author of that particular translation has it wrong.

For years I had vicious nightmares of "escaping hell." The setting for hell was always my childhood home. It wasn't until I "escaped" the addictions and lies of my family that I came to understand these dreams as hopeful. Writing down my nightmares and relating to them like letters from a trusted guide, I realized that they were pointing to a way out. They were telling me that I was not safe in my home and that I needed to get out.

It is okay that some dreams take a while to understand. The value of keeping your dreams in your journals is that often, when you read them at a later time, you come to understand their meanings. You will find that once you receive the hidden message of a recurring dream, you will no longer dream it.

> "What do the characters in your nightmare want? Write about
> that and you will see deeper into your own
> soul and its intentions."
>
> —Kathy Crook, dream guide, wisdomkeeper

To journal your nightmares, first just write them out as you remember them. Then respond to the following questions and suggestions in your journal to gain more insight about their meanings.

> "All the things one
> has forgotten scream
> for help in dreams."
>
> —Elias Canetti,
> Bulgarian author,
> 1981 Nobel laureate

- What repeats in these nightmares?
- What makes you safe in these dreams? Who is the hero or possible hero in these nightmares? Where's the hero found in your dreams?
- Write a short play using the characters and the location of your dream. Is there any part of you that is the mean character?
- What might your soul be trying to tell you? Where is the hope in your dream?
- Write a new ending to your dream.

Off the Page

Make up a video game with the characters and drama of the nightmare. Many writers use their dreams for scenes in their books. Some children's books are known to have been based on someone's dream.

Make a dream catcher. For instructions, Google *dream catcher* or go to your local arts and crafts or bead store for a dream-catcher kit.

Recurring Dreams

One scene I visit repeatedly in my dreams feels like a place I knew well in another lifetime. I live on the ocean and ships are coming and going. The shore is sandy. Next to the shore is a steep hill that goes up to where our village is. From this recurring scene, I imagine an entire life. . . .

I was a man in this life. I was strong, happy, but lonely for family members who were often gone to sea. I had to be one of the men to remain with the village in order to protect it. We were a loving tribe, and safe because of our location on the high ground next to the ocean. We had no neighbors at the time.

To go in the dark with a light is to know the light.
To know the dark, go dark. Go without sight,
and find that the dark, too, blooms and sings,
and is traveled by dark feet and dark wings.

—WENDELL BERRY,
AMERICAN POET,
AUTHOR, ESSAYIST

I enjoyed my life there but often wanted to join the other men out at sea. I was never to go to sea because the men who were protectors of the land and community were forbidden to put their feet on a boat.

❖

* Choose a recurring scene in your dreams. Write about this place. Write about who you were. What happened to you? Add to this dream.
* Turn this dream into a short story or poem.
* How does this repetitive dream speak to your life now?

On the Other Side of the Door

"Thou hast only to follow the wall far enough and there will be a door in it."

—THE DOOR IN THE WALL, MARGUERITE DE ANGELI, AMERICAN AUTHOR OF CHILDREN'S BOOKS

My night dreams and daydreams often overlap. Sometimes I take care of something that's bothering me in my night dreams and my day life is improved. Other times, I daydream (imagine) and write in my journal, and my night dreams shift. During difficult times when I felt as if I was lost in a dark room without a door, my dreams became my door. When I entered that door I would find myself in a different room, a room of possibilities.

You may have to feel along a long dark wall to find the door out of the room you are in. Or your room may be brightly lit with the door in plain sight, ready for you to open it and move through. Find your door and open it, and step into the next room. Use your dreams to discover more about who you are, what you are afraid of; what you want and what you don't want. At the very least, your dreams will give you insight into yourself. And the better you know yourself, the safer and more radiant the world becomes for you.

We usually think of daydreaming as rather aimless, but purposeful daydreaming is a form of creating and a style of meditation. With purposeful daydreaming, you guide your thoughts and ideas and follow where they take you to get an image of how you would like your life and the events in it to progress. Don't mistake ruminating on the past or worrying about the future as purposeful. A purposeful daydream has positive intentions and is creating a picture of how you want your life to be.

> I dream about having lots of money and surprising my sister with a car, then we could take off on road trips. I dream about my father being okay with my sister and I going on road trips together and him being happy in his job. I dream about leaving high school and when I get scared I dream about a better year every time I come back to school, and hope the teachers are decent. I dream about my mother and I getting along better. I dream about traveling and meeting people who are interesting and about not wanting to gossip. I dream that my best friend and I are friends for life and that we go off to college together. I dream most of the time in history class because the teacher is rude and boring. I dream about what I am going to do this weekend.
>
> —LANA, AGE 16

✻ Write about what you daydream about.

✻ Write for five minutes, nonstop, about what the best possible day in your life would look like. Don't worry about trying to be realistic, just write whatever comes.

✻ Write a few sentences on each of the following: perfect-fitting jeans; an encounter with an old friend; a couple of hours of really good writing; something good to eat; receiving a thank you; a surprise phone call.

✻ Now write about the worst day of your life. Again, it can be all true or a mix of fiction and truth.

✻ Write a paragraph for each of the following leads:

   What I want most right now is . . .

I wish I could show you,
When you are lonely or in darkness,
The Astonishing Light
Of your own Being.

—FROM *I HEARD GOD LAUGHING* BY HAFIZ, 14TH-CENTURY PERSIAN SUFI POET AND PHILOSOPHER, TRANSLATED BY DANIEL LADINSKY

Nobody knows this about me, but . . .
I wish I had told my mother that . . .
I often dream about . . .

Rock Writings: Listening to Spirit's Call

The next four entries of this chapter and the paintings of rock art in this chapter are by American artist Geri Schrab. She was inspired to paint on paper the petroglyphs she sees at sites around the world. She understands that this rock art is humanity's first attempt to keep a journal. Here she shares these original messages with us through her art and her own writings. To learn more about Geri's work visit www.artglyphs.com.

Listen to those secret wishes,
Heed those impossible Dreams.

Shaman's Eyes by Geri Schrab, inspired by New Mexico petroglyph site

Spirit loves to fill the Well,
The Heart
that has the courage to Dream.

—**Geri Schrab**

At the time the pursuit of rock art began to call to me, I was unacquainted with the spiritual in my life. I told myself that things we can't see, touch, or measure really don't have much value. Good grades, prospects of a prestigious and well-paying profession—that is how we measure what has value, isn't it? But a little voice kept coming to me, telling me that art is really fun.

I heard this voice when I was in grade school, high school, and then as a young adult already working in a "practical" profession, thinking of going back to school yet again. I had an ongoing argument with myself: "Art makes me happy. But my job is good and secure (and depressing) and pays the bills quite well." My true calling, this passion and connection with rock art, came to me when I reached my late thirties! I had the typical adult responsibilities and NO art education. What could I (or Spirit?) possibly be thinking? Art is for special people, after all. Certainly that couldn't be me.

Everything began to change when I saw my first "rock art" site. Petroglyphs and pictographs carved and painted on the rock faces by the people indigenous to this land spoke to the part of me that my day job was trying to put to sleep. The drawings reached out to me across time and invited me to create. Those mysterious ancient images called to me. I stared at my photos of that first site for nearly a year. . . . The dance with Spirit had begun, but I just didn't know it yet.

Then I found myself asking, "Hmmmm, wonder if I can paint something like that?"

That was about ten years ago. I no longer have that job that zapped the life out of me. I do still have the day-to-day responsibilities. Now, I have not only a very healthy, growing collection of paintings of those petroglyphs and pictographs, but also a beautiful collection of wonderful people all across the country who buy them because my work nourishes their spirits, as well.

You just never know what will happen when you quiet yourself, trust what calls you, and act courageously—because Spirit loves the heart that dares to feel and mobilize its impossible dreams.

✱ Write about impossible dreams.
✱ Write about what calls you.
✱ Write about that little voice inside of you.
✱ Look at the rock images in this chapter. Write a story about them. What are they saying?
✱ Write about having fun.

Off the Page

Visiting a Rock Art Site

When you visit a sacred place such as a site with ancient rock art, you access Spirit at a profound and timeless level. Although pictographs are commonly called "rock art," they probably weren't intended as art at all, but recordings of stories, journeys, hunts, and visions; in essence, the history of the indigenous people. They are their journals! Let's honor their history and meaning by "reading" them and walking softly at these sites.

The magic of visiting these sites, for me, came through the back door; I was unaware of their sacred nature at the time they came into my life. Now that I've been working with them for ten years, I seek them out. I go to places that are known to be or feel sacred, to replenish my spirit with the good energy of those who have gone before and of the natural places in which the sites are found.

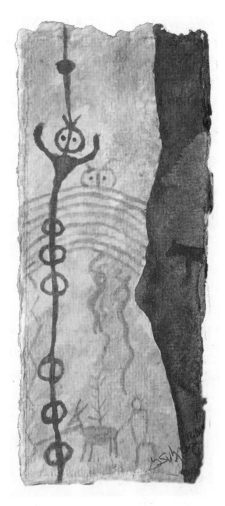

Spirit Sees by Geri Schrab, inspired by Utah petroglyph site

"It is good to
remember that each
of us has a different
dream."

—CROW NATION WISDOM

Visiting and studying the rock art left behind by the ancestors offers us a doorway to another world where we can learn about and understand the ancient Native people. When you visit a sacred site, it is good to ask Spirit for permission to visit. Be aware of its sacredness, honor it, and pay attention while you are there. These sites should be visited with the same respect you would show in a synagogue, temple, or church. Say thank you as you leave.

"All dreams spin out
from the same web."

—HOPI PROVERB

Recognizing the Language of Your Soul

Learning to feel and know your own unique language of spirit opens a doorway to your own center and soul. For me it was in the messages of night dreams, daydreams, the rock art sites, and my paintings that I recognized the language of my soul. Through my art and dreams I heard what Spirit was telling me, and it always felt right to follow its message. I have found it helps to approach my own communication with Spirit with the same reverence I hold for any other sacred place. When I visit the sacred sites within me through my art, I know I am visiting a holy place and I open myself up to this. And I respond to rock art not only by painting what I see and experience but by writing my emotions, insights, and experiences into my journal. My journal then becomes another sacred site to visit and learn from.

Through your dreams, your journals, oracles, or your own art you will discover a very real connection to the spirit within you and outside of you. Look for and learn your own language of spirit. It is expressed through your unique visions and dreams, and they will become a sacred place of communication for you.

✻ Write about your sacred places. What makes them sacred? What do they say to you that draws you back?

✻ How is your journal a sacred site?

✻ Write about the image *Spirit Sees* on page 53—what does it say to you?

Off the Page

Visit a site that you consider sacred and journal about the experience afterward. Although most sacred sites I visit are rock art sites, there are many other kinds of places to experience the sacred. There are mounds, shrines, temples, churches, ancient trees, and favorite lakes. Even that clump of willows you loved to hide under when you were a little kid can be sacred. If it anchors you to your source of spirit and allows communication with your spiritual source, it is a sacred place indeed. (See chapter 6 for more about the sacred in nature.)

Soul Vandalism

One of the saddest things I have come across in this work is vandalism at these sacred sites. Many sites have had initials carved on them, and art has been scratched off, shot at, painted over with spray paint, and even cut out and stolen. Although the center and focus of my work, the spark, is painting images from the rock art sites I visit, this has led to many other interests. Among them is the desire to help educate the public not to perpetrate damage on such sites, and to help clean it up when it does happen. An unexpected result of this work is that it began to "clean up" me.

Rock art vandalism photographed by Geri Schrab

Just like a rock art site that had been painted upon, my own soul had been vandalized for years. Perhaps this is true for you too. Just like the damage at rock art sites, such damage is not always purposefully done; sometimes it is the result of lack of understanding and awareness. Many times the graffiti seems small and unimportant, but the damage is big. Like what happened to me in sixth grade when I made a special painting that I was excited to show my teacher—who looked at it and didn't say a thing. This silence made me feel ashamed of my art. Sometimes, unfortunately, the vandalism to our hearts is really malicious and does significant damage. Sometimes we carve the wound in ever deeper with negative messages to ourselves.

A nasty truth about graffiti at rock art sites is that vandalism begets more vandalism. Once people see graffiti carved upon a site, they feel that it's okay for them to add their own. By the same token, once your soul has been vandalized in a certain way, it may seem to you that that's the way it should be, and you learn to allow it to be vandalized by others. Or you may do as I did, retracing those negative messages to harm yourself further. It was a very hard lesson for me, to learn to plant my boundaries, respect myself, and say, No—it is not okay to carve your initials here. *I like my spirit just the way it is.*

Regardless of how your own personal "soul vandalism" happened, the most important element in the equation at this point is you. Even though someone may have purposely sprayed paint over your heart or carved their hurtful initials in your soul, by understanding and working with the voice of your loving spirit, you can heal that damage. Eventually your soul will feel really good and its beautiful true messages will shine through.

* Write about who did the damage in "Rock art vandalism" on page 55.
* Write about negative messages vandalizing your soul. What unwanted "graffiti" has confused your clear message as it tries to come through?
* What types of vandalism do you perpetrate on yourself?
* What is the message underneath, from your true self, that shines through? Write about that.
* What are the loving messages you hear but sometimes toss away? Journal about them. And then journal about them again. And again. All the good ones. Carving those in deeply is a good thing.

Off the Page

In what activity or pastime does Spirit talk most clearly to you? Is it through writing, painting, throwing a pot, playing an instrument, singing a song, throwing a baseball, planting a garden, weeding a garden? Spend time doing something that can help you work that "vandalism" out.

"Cruelty cannot stop the earth's heart from beating."

—FROM *TO BE A DRUM* BY EVELYN COLEMAN, AMERICAN WRITER

The Vision of Corn Maiden

Corn Maiden by Geri Schrab, inspired by Utah petroglyph site

This painting came at a time of personal crisis for me. An emotional injury I suffered nearly tore me not only from my dream, but from life itself. It was difficult to regain my equilibrium because it seemed I no longer understood or heard my own voice of Spirit. I lost the connection with spirit and with my self that I had found through the rock art. I began to lose touch with everything good. I was frightened but still I searched for my art. I searched for my self.

Corn Maiden was very difficult to create.

When this painting finally came to me it spoke (it gave me a vision) and woke my soul back up. It told me, "No matter what your perception of who or what caused the hurt, *Always Sow Good Seeds*." I could hear this voice deep inside my being, "No matter what, always sow good seeds." This sowing of seeds, I realized, is where all the new beginnings will originate. What I am germinating may take a while, but I know it will be good because the seeds are strong. The seeds are of kindness and hope. Corn Maiden teaches me, and your art or passion can teach you, that we do indeed reap what we sow. I am not going to sow more pain and anger into the soil of my soul.

With this Corn Maiden painting my language of Spirit found its voice again. And the paint flows freely. And I thank Spirit for this vision and I am grateful.

✦

✳ Write about what the image of Corn Maiden elicits in you.
✳ Write about karma.
✳ What do you need to return to?
✳ Write about being grateful.

Consulting Oracles for Direction

An oracle, such as the I Ching or tarot, is a means by which you can consult spirit and deities. This medium allows you to be in communication with your spiritual source. Consulting it on a regular basis also increases your intuitive abilities.

*Dreams and
Oracles*

60

There are many great resources and books on oracles. The oracle I use and journal about is the I Ching. The I Ching is an ancient book of timeless wisdom expressed in the form of sixty-four hexagrams that can help the inquirer with guidance on day-to-day concerns. This ancient Chinese oracle guided me through my teen and adult years, and I attribute much of my happiness and success to its wisdom. I wrote a guide to the I Ching (*I Ching for Teens*) because I know how helpful such a resource can be. Other oracles include rune stones, the tarot, genuine indigenous elders (shamans), labyrinths, pendulums, and even nature itself. Of course there are many card decks out there that you can consult—animal medicine cards, goddess cards, and angel cards, to name a few. You will want to find the one that fits for you.

How you relate to your oracle will determine what you get out of it. This, of course, is true of all of our relationships. What we put in is what we get out. For this reason being aware of your intentions when you approach an oracle is essential.

I begin my consultation with the I Ching by writing in my journal about the issue that concerns me and about whatever is surrounding this concern. This includes pretty much anything of importance that is going on in my life at the time. After I am finished journaling I write out my question for the I Ching. I try to get as specific as possible, so the I Ching and I are clear about what I am focusing on. This will make the oracle's response much clearer.

Then, before I toss the I Ching coins (or use my handmade I Ching cards), I phrase my question so: "Please comment on the nature of the situation and on the attitude and action I should follow at this time." This wording or something like it prepares you for the kind of answer an oracle will provide. You may want to write it in your journal but after a while you will likely have it memorized.

In choosing your oracle it is important that you find one that is compatible with your spiritual beliefs and brings you messages of hope and insight. The I Ching, for example, is not attached to any particular religious sect, and people from many spiritual backgrounds consider it beneficial. Find one that resonates with your spiritual practice so that it will deepen this relationship with your spiritual source.

What have you been told about oracles such as the tarot?

I always thought the tarot was related to devil worshipers. I am not sure where I got that one. Then I checked into it because my best friend got a deck for her seventeenth birthday from her aunt. There is a devil card in there but it is not about devils and demons. The devil card, it turns out, represents our negative self-talk, our worries, and our "dark" side. My friend's aunt said that some religions "demonize" others' beliefs because what others believe makes them uncomfortable.

—RIVER, AGE 17, WHO NOW CONSULTS THE TAROT REGULARLY

To get the most out of your relationship with your oracle you will want to write your questions and response in your journal. I've kept a record of my I Ching consultations from the age of sixteen—which of course provided me with plenty of material when I wrote my I Ching book at the age of forty-six.

* Write about your deity.
* Write a list of questions you might want to consult an oracle about.

> ## Off the Page
>
> Give yourself some time to learn about and choose an oracle. Go to my Web site for information on the I Ching; check out *Tarot for Teens* by M. J. Abadie; go to your local bookstore (particularly independent ones that specialize in spiritual books and resources) and look over their various divination decks. Read up on consulting a pendulum. Check out my books *Teen Psychic* and *I Ching for Teens*.

"The best mind-altering drug is truth."

—WRITTEN BY JANE WAGNER FOR LILY TOMLIN

The Power of Attention and Intention

The I Ching, also called the Book of Changes, is known to be at least two thousand years old. Is ancient wisdom better than modern wisdom? Think about sacred sites (like the ones previously mentioned). What makes them sacred? Have they always been sacred? In reality, what part of Mother Earth is not sacred? It is the attention and respect that we have brought to these places over and over again that empowered them and made them sacred.

Whatever you repetitively bring your attention to becomes your link to the sacred and at the same time empowers it. When you keep directing your positive attention to an oracle, such as the I Ching, a very real and dynamic relationship occurs. You get valid responses to your questions that help you in the real world.

Attention is the physical manifestation of love. Whatever receives your positive attention and energy becomes sacred. The more you consult the oracle of your choice, the more wisdom and strength you will glean from it. So in order to benefit from your chosen oracle you need to bring your attention to it on a regular basis. Then you need to hold the intention of practicing its principles.

Once you bring your attention to your oracle you need to be honest and clear about your intentions. The I Ching, for example, is full of wisdom and principles that can help you with every issue that arises in your life. But the Sage (spirit wisdomkeeper and voice of the I Ching) knows *you* are ultimately the cause of your life. Regularly consulting an oracle only reinforces your understanding of this reality. You need to agree to seriously consider your oracle's guidance and base your behaviors and thoughts on what it suggests.

When you bring your attention regularly to an oracle or sacred site or holy text, you will bring its principles into your life and be empowered by them.

✳ What are you *not* giving your attention to? Your pet? Your room? Your friends, your job, your journal, your sport, your art? How does this influence the relationship? Write about this.

✳ What gets your attention on a regular basis?

✳ Write about some of your personal principles.

Off the page

Practice Mindfulness Meditation (see pages 230–31) to strengthen your ability to direct your attention. Do the Pebble Meditation (What is my true nature?) on page 69, making the question "Where is my attention?"

"The I Ching is probably one of the most important books of the world, because the two branches of Chinese philosophy, Confucianism and Taoism, have common root in the I Ching. It emphasizes eternal values in the middle of a continually changing universe, assumes a cosmos that has a discernible underlying pattern, and strongly advises holding to inner principles through which it may be possible to learn to live in harmony with the Tao, the invisible meaning-giving matrix of the universe."

—FROM *THE TAO OF PSYCHOLOGY* BY JEAN SHINODA BOLEN, M.D., JUNGIAN PSYCHOANALYST

"Genius is nothing but continued attention."

—HELVETIUS, 18TH-CENTURY FRENCH PHILOSOPHER

Trustworthy oracles can be expected to include principles such as these:

- You are responsible for your own happiness.
- Everything and everyone has an innate sacred timing.
- Trust your own intuition and creativity.
- Expect and embrace change.
- Cultivate inner independence.
- You reap what you sow. (Often referred to as "karma.")
- There is an underlying and unifying reality in life; everyone and everything is connected. (This concept is often expressed as "the Tao.")

In consulting oracles it is important to remember that the guidance you receive will not be about changing the outside circumstances of your life; instead, it will bring attention to what needs to be addressed in your internal world.

Journaling with Your Oracle

While you are writing your question and consulting your oracle, notice your thoughts and feelings—these will be significant as you seek to understand the meaning of your reading. A growing trust of your own intuitive wisdom comes forth the more you consult your oracle with this awareness. Intuitively you will come to understand very quickly what the oracle is teaching you. This is again the power of returned attention—your ability to interpret its message increases with each visit. By recording your concerns and the results of your consultations in your journal to look over later, you will further develop your ability to interpret and act on the oracle's wisdom.

What the I Ching has taught me is to trust myself more. I was always so afraid and hesitant about everything. Gradually, after months and months of consult—

ing I Ching for Teens, I have come to notice just how much is in my power to change. It all begins with me. And it is all recorded in my journal.

—ANITA, AGE 18

* Journal for five minutes on what concerns you today.
* Choose a question from the entry you just wrote. Now, using whatever oracle suits you, present the question and read the response. What does the message of the oracle's reading point to?
* Paraphrase the message of the reading in one pithy phrase for yourself, using your own words.
* Write about the blind leading the blind.
* Write about trust.

Chocolate Soup: Symbolic Sight

When you find yourself bored or wanting something to do, look around you for metaphors—look at the world *symbolically*. Take some time to notice all the metaphors that are living and moving around you. Right now. This is a way to open up to the present moment and develops your symbolic sight.

For young children this is a natural skill, until too much schooling tends to take it away. My daughter is eight and school hasn't yet penetrated her ability to see and experience life metaphorically and magically. She doesn't see things as they *are;* she sees things as she *experiences* them. She still experiences life as an unfolding story. (And this is what life is for all of us, all the time—a story wanting to unfold.) For my daughter, hot chocolate is "chocolate soup." For my daughter, cars have souls and need to be talked to before you get into them. For her, the prairie of fireflies is a garden of wild light and fairies.

Our walk down the driveway to the school bus every morning is a small adventure in which we encounter coyote footprints, share conversations about why fairies are small (they have their reasons,

Dreams and Oracles

*Dreams and
Oracles*

of course), greet our three visiting cranes, and talk about our hopes for the day. As we walk we are confronting the empty page of an entire day—and all the possibilities it may hold. As we walk I get to practice my symbolic sight. Life is experienced spiritually through this symbolic sight—I see the cranes carrying a message from Spirit as they call out to us: "Look, see, hear—Spirit is everywhere."

* Write about the following and give them symbolic meaning:
    a fly in your soup
    a double rainbow
    an encounter with a crow
    a car accident in which no one was hurt
* Rise with the morning sun (a most sacred act). Let the first rays of the sun shine on you, your day, and your journal. Then spend ten minutes writing under the rising sun.
* Write about the moon in the day sky.
* Write about an everyday miracle.
* Write about coincidences.

Off the Page

Experience this day as a story, full of images and messages from the spirit world unfolding in every moment—symbols and metaphors everywhere. Carry this openness with you through the day (journal in hand), being receptive to all possibilities. This openness to symbolic sight will read as an invitation to the spirit world to fill your day up with meaning.

4

Knowing Your True Nature through Writing

Wisdom

Words of wise men
scatter
through centuries of voices
Sounding
as stars
in the night sky
speaking
constellations of light
Until
some bright new star
appears

altering relations.

—SHANNON KING, POET, ARTIST

"Say not, 'I have found the truth,' but
rather, 'I have found *a* truth.'
Say not, 'I have found the path of the soul.'
Say rather, 'I have met the soul walking upon my path.'
For the soul walks upon all paths.
The soul walks not upon a line, neither
does it grow like a reed.
The soul unfolds itself, like a lotus of countless petals."

—From *The Prophet* by Kahlil Gibran,
Lebanese-American poet and mystic

"Be patient toward all that is unsolved in your heart and try to
love the questions themselves."

—Rainer Maria Rilke, Czech poet

"What Is My True Nature?" A Meditation

Writing is a primary way to be open to your truest self. When you write you merge with so much more than you may appreciate at the time. Notice how you feel inside your body after you are done writing a poem, a letter to a loved one, a prose piece, or an idea in your journal. The soul loves to write, to see itself on paper, in a dance of words and images.

Writing allows you time to give attention to your soul, and for your soul to speak to you. Buddhists call the soul our original or true nature; Quakers call it the inner teacher or the inner light; some traditions refer to it as the soul; Hindus refer to it as the Brahman. As a therapist I often refer to it as your true self, or your essential nature. Writing in your journal will bring forth this inner light and increase your inner independence and self-esteem. Your entire world may say no or drive your truth into hiding, but in your journal your truth emerges and therefore cannot be quieted.

Of course you may wonder, "What is my true nature?" "How can I bring forth my inner light when I am not writing in my journal?"

"In its silence
it speaks . . .
wholeness . . . and
integrity that comes
from being what
you are."

—Douglas Wood,
Australian engineer,
entrepreneur

"Who is the real me?" Practicing the following meditation will help you with those questions. Give yourself at least ten minutes to do this meditation and write in your journal.

Pebble Meditation

Sit in a chair with your feet on the floor, comfortable, yet alert. Close your eyes. Rest for a few minutes in your breathing. Then ask yourself the question "What is my true nature?" Drop this question into the middle of your consciousness like a pebble dropping into the center of a still pond, and let the question gently ripple out . . . throughout your being. . . .

"What is my true nature?"

For another moment, relax in your breathing . . . letting the ripples move out. Sit in the stillness of this question. . . .

Then return your attention to your feet on the floor. Either open your eyes and begin to journal or take this time now to do a ten-minute Mindfulness (breath) Meditation (see pages 230–31).

* Write about your true self.
* What is essential about you?
* Write about feeling like a fake.
* Write about what you would do if you were guaranteed not to fail.
* Have an argument between your false self and your true self. What do they fight about?

The Seed of the True Self

"What seed was planted when you or I arrived on earth with our identities intact?" Parker Palmer, author and educator, asks this question of his readers in *A Hidden Wholeness*. He invites us to remember and reclaim our "birthright gifts and potentials."

"What we achieve inwardly will change outer reality."

—OTTO RANK,
GERMAN PSYCHOLOGIST,
THEOLOGIAN

Knowing Your
True Nature
through Writing

69

From my training in psychology I know that we are either developing our true nature—a true self—or we are developing a false self. The false self is often set up only to please others, to not question, to do what is comfortable (but not necessarily safe), to go with the crowd. The true self, by contrast, has compassion for others but does not set out to make everyone happy; is safe but often uncomfortable because it is dynamic and changing; is unique and does not typically just go with the crowd. This development of our true or false self can begin at a young age—so why not choose to develop your true self now? As a psychotherapist for twenty-five years, I worked with many people who fought off their true nature until one day—WHAM!—it seemed to hit them over the head. "Here I am!" it shouted. Why wait? Why not begin to build a life on what is true for you *now*?

Every writing exercise in this book has the potential to help you develop your true nature. Every moment you bring your self honestly to the journal and write, you are developing your true self. As I have written elsewhere, the greatest gift you can bring to the world is your self—your true self.

- ✱ Write about what you dreamed of being when you were five, eight, ten, and twelve.
- ✱ What is false about you?
- ✱ Write about being true to yourself.
- ✱ Pretend you are forty years old. Write a letter to yourself.
- ✱ Imagine yourself just born; you are being held lovingly by your mother or father. You feel this love throughout your entire body. Now write about your potential.
- ✱ Write about your true self, using the following words as prompts: *clear, not until, birthright, true enough, now.*

Awaken the Shakti

In the West, we tend to think of the creative force as a masculine characteristic, while the feminine is seen as receptive and quiet. But in the Hindu tradition, these associations are reversed. The goddess Shakti (literally translated as "power") is the creative force. So creative is she in yogic myth that she created the world. Her partner, the god Shiva, is her quiet supporter.

Each of us is made up of both the shakti and shiva energies. They are complementary, and when both are in balance our lives are more creative and joyful. Practice the following meditation to awaken the shakti, and to balance the two vital energies. Begin by taking a few minutes to ground (see pages 231–32).

Sit in a meditative posture on the floor or in a chair with your feet on the floor. For about ten breaths, begin to rest your awareness on the physical sensation of breathing. After these ten breaths, bring your awareness down to the bottom of your spine. Imagine there a small fire smoldering there. In your imagination, use your inhalations to fan the fire, and watch it slowly rise up your spine, up to the top of your head. Once it has reached the top or crown of your head, move the heat of the fire back downward, along the front of your head and torso, meeting back up with its source at the spine's root. Sit and breathe for a few minutes, noticing the shakti energy waking you up.

Notice what you are feeling and, when you are ready, journal about these sensations and this experience.

* Write about feeling intense.
* Write about something remarkable.
* Write about a time you or someone you were with lost control.

Your True Name

Have you already changed your name, or added to it somehow? Do you have a "nickname" you feel represents more closely who you are? Renaming yourself is one way to express your increased inner independence. In many cultures, one would traditionally receive his or her spiritual name when initiated into adulthood, which would be during adolescence. Lacking such a tradition in our culture, some of us simply choose a name that feels more like who we are. Your true name may come from your own soul through a dream or vision, or a sense of "knowing" that this is a truer name for you. Or it may be bestowed on you by a spiritual elder, someone who has a solid reputation for being a reliable and knowledgeable spiritual guide.

For the next couple of weeks, watch your dreams. Ask for your dreams to show you your true name. Pay attention to synchronicities. These too may be pointing to a true name.

I thought about a name and for some reason "Flowering Rabbit Hopper" came to mind. I am a rabbit in the Chinese Zodiac so rabbits have always had a place in my heart. I also feel like I'm hopping through my life in the world, trying to discover—sort of like a rabbit. Right now my life is flowering, blooming with the new experiences that I am encountering and will soon be encountering on the many trips I am taking this summer. I'm going to be heading to college in the fall—a new life opening.

—AMANDA, AGE 18

- ✶ Write the story of your nickname.
- ✶ Write about a time you were misunderstood.
- ✶ What animal represents you? Include this animal in your true name.
- ✶ Choose a spirit name for yourself.

Knowing Your True Nature through Writing

72

Where Is Your Mind?

The beautiful thing about journals is that they are written for you—no one else. I also write my books this way. I don't sit down and think, "I have to please my readers." Instead I sit and write what wants to write through me. I may have the reader in mind, but I write for myself first—especially in my journals.

I suggest you also write for yourself first. If you plan on getting published, your rewrites can be done with the reader in mind. But when you begin writing, you have to clear your mind the best you can of all its clutter so the creativity has room to move through you. This is one reason I begin my day with a meditation practice. Stilling my busy, planning, crazy mind allows a space for the creative juices to flow.

What is it you typically have your attention on? Whatever you give your attention to is what is going to grow and become real in your life. Really being aware of where your attention is gives you the ability to create your life. The ability to guide your thinking, your attention, will be a skill that will empower your creative side and set you free. Your mind is not always an ally in this. It is more like a wild monkey that you need to tame. Too often the mind is full of unnecessary or negative thoughts.

You can, when you choose, learn how to direct your thoughts—and as a result, create a life. Meditation is a simple practice of quieting the mind by focusing your attention on your breath. Many events in life will attempt to throw you off center. With meditation and journaling practice you can learn to stay centered and focused (present) even during the more difficult times. Learning to "return to the breath" will help you place your attention where you really want it. Writing itself is a form of meditation—while I am writing I am focused on the subject that matters to me. My attention is on my writing, and nothing gets between me and the paper.

"We move forward and become that which we think about. Isn't it time we began to think about what we're thinking about?"

—DON COYHIS, MOHICAN COMMUNITY BUILDER AND WISDOMKEEPER

Knowing Your True Nature through Writing

Try this: Focus your attention for a couple of moments entirely on a spot on your body (it can be on your skin or on your clothes). Breathe naturally while focusing your attention on that one place on your body. Now shift your focus from that spot and find a place on the wall to bring your full attention to. Now for a few moments, breathing naturally, keep your full attention on that spot on the wall. . . . Again, return your focus to a spot on your body; for a few moments place your full attention on that spot on your clothing or body. Breathe naturally. Now once again, take your attention outward and place your full attention on some spot on the wall. Breathe and focus.

This practice shows us how we can direct our attention where we choose—when we choose.

* What did you observe about this experience?
* Every hour on the hour, notice and jot down in a pocket journal where your attention is. (Or just carry a scrap of paper in your pocket.) Where are your thoughts focusing? Every time you look at the clock (and in school you probably do this a lot), notice where your attention is. Is it in the moment? Is it on something you are going to do after school? Is it on something you overheard in the hallway? Is it on a feeling you are having? Write this down in your journal. Begin to notice more and more where you are putting your attention—and, therefore, your energy.
* Write about getting someone's attention.
* Write about what gets your attention.
* I lost interest when . . .

As You Wish

—A traditional folktale, oral tradition, source unknown.
Retold by Julie Tallard Johnson

There was once a young woman, about the age of twenty-one, who thought that "this spiritual stuff" was nonsense and a waste of time. She believed that those who claim to have wisdom are fooling everyone.

Not too far away, a wise woman lived in a hut at the top of a very high mountain. She was known to be a sage and could answer the most difficult questions about life. People from far and wide would travel to seek her counsel. She was considered a truthteller.

But the young woman doubted the sage's ability. She bragged to her friends that she could trick the old sage and confuse her. This would show everyone that the old woman was a fake! The young woman held in her hand a little chickadee and told her friends, "I'll climb the mountain and find this wise woman, and when I do I will hold this little chickadee behind my back. I'll ask her if the bird is alive or dead. If she says dead, I will bring the bird out and show her that the bird is alive. If she says alive I will crush it quietly with my hands behind my back and bring it out and show her that it is dead."

With that intention she climbed to the top of the mountain and searched for the wise woman. When she found the hut, she called out, "Old woman! Old woman!"

A quiet voice answered from behind the closed door, "What is it you want my daughter?"

"I have a question for you." She hid the bird behind her back.

The old woman spoke from behind the door, "Then ask me, my daughter."

The young woman smiled at her own cleverness and said, "Behind my back, I have a little bird in my hands. I want to know if the bird is alive or dead."

After a few moments of deep silence, the old sage replied in a weary voice, "It is as you wish, my daughter."

Knowing Your True Nature through Writing

Off the Page

Do the Grounding Meditation described on pages 231–32.
When you feel grounded ask yourself, What does my body
want?
What does my soul need?
Journal your answers.

Ride the Wave of Breath

Wave Mandala
Drawing by Arline Beagan

This particular meditation is good for relaxation, to help you prepare for sleep, or to unwind the mind when it is anxious. An object to focus on visually can help you to relax your attention on one thing and let go of worries and stress. Anxiety, stress, and worries will cover over your true nature like a cloud blocks the sun. It's not wrong to feel anxious, but if you remain masked in anxiety for too long the light of your essential self will be hidden. Water is a particularly good image for "washing away" stress and anxiety. So use this meditation, with the illustration on the opposite page, to wash away your worries like releasing the rain out of the cloud. This lets your true nature shine through. Give yourself five minutes to practice this meditation and then at least five more minutes to journal.

Use the wave mandala to focus your attention. Rest your eyes on the image of the mandala. . . . Breathe in. . . . Breathe out. . . . Hold a gentle gaze on the wave mandala as you continue to breathe deeply. Feel the wave come in and wash its calmness over you; and then feel it wash out into the great ocean with all your stresses and difficulties. Breathe in calmness and breathe out stress . . . riding the wave. Breathe in. . . . Breathe out. . . . Breathe in calmness, breathe out stress.

Tonight, before you go to sleep, take a moment and rest your eyes gently on the wave mandala and imagine the waves coming in and calming you, and the waves going out, washing away your worries and stresses. Let your breath just breathe through you, calming you as you breathe in and breathe out. Know that the great ocean can easily absorb all and any negativity. Sleep well and deeply.

* Write about the ocean.
* Write about riding a wave.
* Write about a thunderstorm.
* Write about a good night's sleep.

"Your own mind is a sacred enclosure into which nothing harmful can enter except by your permission."

—ARNOLD BENNETT, ENGLISH JOURNALIST, NOVELIST

Knowing Your True Nature through Writing

Zen Garden: A Good Lazy

Looking at the photo below, rest your eyes softly on the center of the water while you breathe. Hold a soft, lazy focus on the image

A Zen garden

and open up to the natural feeling it offers you. Allow the water streaming into the pool to calm you. No thoughts—just gentle attention on the image.

Water reminds you of how you can be fluid and flexible with your life. Let yourself open up fully to the moment by being like water, allowing the moment to shape you. Be like water in a stressful situation—give yourself permission to relax into it, rather than trying to shape it, or force something. This is a good laziness, in which you let go, relax, and open yourself up. Bring this image of the Zen garden to mind when you are feeling overwhelmed this week.

❖

Imagine yourself sitting in the Zen garden; hear the water drip and feel the soft, warm breeze move the small hairs on your arm. Feel its gentleness envelop you. . . .

* Write as if you were the Buddhist monk in the Zen garden. What wisdom does the garden hold for you?
* Write about being called lazy.
* Ralph Waldo Emerson, American poet, transcendental philosopher, and author of many published journals, wrote, "The hero is the person who is immovably centered." What does he mean by this?

Self, Meet Self

"That is my essential reason for writing, not for fame, not to be celebrated after death, but to heighten and create life all around me. I also write because when I am writing I reach the high moment of fusion sought by the mystics, the poets, the lovers, a sense of communion with the universe."

—FROM *THE DIARY OF ANAÏS NIN 1939–1944*
BY ANAÏS NIN, FRENCH AUTHOR AND DIARIST

Through journaling you can discover a lot about yourself. It is sad, but many people go through their teen years and beyond clueless

"Nothing you will do will make a difference if you can't face the solitude."

—TOM ROBBINS,
AMERICAN NOVELIST
AND STORYTELLER

as to who they are and what they want. You may know an adult who makes comments such as, "I really don't know how I got here," referring to their job or their general situation in life. The more you know about yourself, the more your life will become your own, and the less likely it is that you will be heard saying, "I don't know how I got here."

In my day-to-day life, with its sometimes extreme ups and downs, I can forget myself. I may lose my voice and my way when external events get crazy. My journals have been my "voice," reminding me who I am and what I want to become. I return to my journals to find myself, my intentions, my spiritual voice. They don't let me forget my dreams (of writing books, traveling); they don't let me forget my spiritual intentions (to live compassionately and creatively); they don't let me forget who I am. With this reminder, I am never lost for long.

✦

Finish the following simple lines. There are no rules—just write. Be silly, be honest, and write whatever you want.

- ✴ My dream for my future is . . .
- ✴ What really makes me angry is . . .
- ✴ When people talk about me they probably say . . .
- ✴ What really surprises me is . . .
- ✴ I hope that . . .
- ✴ I am afraid that . . .
- ✴ What is most spiritual for me is . . .
- ✴ I am happiest when . . .
- ✴ My answer to the question "Who am I?" is . . .
- ✴ The best thing that has happened to me so far is . . .

Guru Meditation

In Tibetan Buddhism and other traditions you call on the image and energies of your deity, saint, or spiritual master to bring forth your true nature. You resonate with the beautiful and balanced energy of your spiritual source to bring forth what is inherent in you. I love the idea of having the same "vibration" as Padmasambhava, the guru of compassion. Guru meditation, also called guru yoga, gives you a very real synergy with an outer teacher to link you up with the truth inside you, your inner teacher. There are entire books on guru yoga because it is a sure way to feel the beauty and spiritual energies inside you. In this practice you allow the energies of your spiritual source into you, lighting up your truth and filling up your heart with Jesus, or the Buddha, or Mother Nature—whatever spiritual teacher really speaks to you. You can follow this up with a five- to ten-minute silent meditation.

Sit quietly. Invoke from the depths of your heart the embodiment of truth in the person of your spiritual master, saint, or enlightened being. Trust that this presence is with you.

Open your heart and allow it to fill with your teacher's presence. Call upon him or her with these words: "Guide me, inspire me, calm my mind, and help me realize my true nature." Give yourself completely to your spiritual teacher. Imagine yourself opening your heart and mind to this teacher.

Say a prayer, or sing a chant.

Allow all the energy from your spiritual teacher to radiate into your being, filling you up. Imagine rays of light coming from the heart of your teacher into you. These rays of light fill you up. This is considered the "empowerment"—the deity is empowering you with his or her energy. In vibrational medicine this means that you will be vibrating at the same level as your spiritual source. Know that taking time to be with your spiritual source will help bring forth your truest and best self.

Become one with this deity, merging yourself completely with him or her. Sit in meditation completely infused with your great teacher.

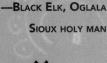

"In a circle the center is always present, and it attracts your eye, whether it is marked or not. The capacity of the circle to catch and focus your attention means that you take less notice of what is outside the circle."

—FROM *COLORING MANDALAS* BY SUSANNE F. FINCHER, JUNGIAN PSYCHOLOGIST, ART THERAPIST

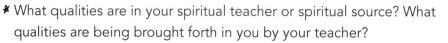

* What qualities are in your spiritual teacher or spiritual source? What qualities are being brought forth in you by your teacher?
* Write about your experience when first practicing this Guru Meditation.
* What does it mean to be "enlightened"?
* Write about a spiritually inspiring person you would like to meet.

Off the Page

Learn some Lakota songs or other Native American chants that are used in healing ceremonies or to call on the energies of the ancestors. Learn one song in its native language. Singing in the language of the indigenous people in the place where they lived is said to call up potent energies. It is also the language the Earth understands. For example, when you sing Native American chants in America, the Earth and the ancestors will hear you; chants sung in Tibet in the Tibetan native language will be heard by the land and ancestors there. What is the local Native language of the place where you live or a place you plan to visit?

Beauty and Wholeness: Your Personal Mandala

In Sanskrit, the ancient language of India, the word *mandala* means "sacred circle." In the Tibetan language the word for mandala, *Kyilkor,* means "center and circumference." Circles represent something sacred in many spiritual traditions—the shape of a gathering for ceremony, the shape of father sun and mother moon. In Egyptian myth a circle is used to create the world. In Native American tradition everything sacred takes place in a circle.

The influential psychoanalyst Carl Jung introduced Western civilization to the value of mandalas for psychological and spiritual healing. He knew that we all want to fulfill our own unique design in life—to live our true nature, and to experience our wholeness. Mandalas express and symbolize our true nature and its wholeness.

> "Mandalas arise from the compelling human need to know our own inner reality, to align this knowing with our body's wisdom, and to awaken in ourselves a sense of being in harmony with the Universe."
> —SUSANNE F. FINCHER, JUNGIAN PSYCHOLOGIST,
> ART THERAPIST, AND AUTHOR OF *COLORING MANDALAS*

In the next four exercises you will create your own mandala. To begin you will need white card stock (poster size is ideal) and markers or crayons. To draw the mandala, place a large round plate in the middle of the paper and trace its outline to make a circle. Now divide the mandala into even quarters by drawing a vertical line and a horizontal line through the center.

Each of the following exercises focuses on one quarter of the mandala. Give yourself an entire week to complete the mandala. The actual time you spend on it will range from two to four hours, depending on the travel time needed for the third exercise. This is a great activity to do in a group.

⊚

First Mandala Exercise

Begin by doing this Lotus Meditation. This meditation is borrowed from the yogic tradition. It helps slow the mind, calm your entire being, promote a sense of serenity, and bring you into the present moment. It will open you up to the truth about you.

Find a quiet place where you can meditate for at least five minutes. Sit in a meditative posture with your eyes closed. Let your breath be relaxed; let it

"For in one soul are contained the hopes and feelings of all mankind."

—KAHLIL GIBRAN, LEBANESE-AMERICAN POET, PHILOSOPHER, MYSTIC

breathe by itself. . . . Bring your awareness down to your belly. Imagine that your lower body is a rich, dark soil. Breathe and imagine . . . then picture a beautiful white lotus flower growing out of this rich soil, growing up through your upper body, and coming to bloom in your heart. Breathe and feel the beauty and the energy of this most sacred flower.

Feel your readiness to bring forth what is within you. Feel the truth of who you are. After you have sat with this truth for a few minutes, you can consult the lotus for guidance. Breathe into the lotus and look into its center. Look into the blossom of the lotus.

Ask this question of the lotus: What does my soul want me to manifest now, today? *Breathe and allow, trust what comes. What's next? What's now? What wants my attention? Breathe.*

Now fill in one quarter of the mandala with colors. Draw only images, no words.

Second Mandala Exercise

For this exercise you will need a few favorite magazines. You will also need glue and scissors (or you may choose to tear instead of cut).

Go through the magazines and randomly cut or tear out pages. Try not to deliberately pick pages, just cut or tear until you have at least thirty-five loose pages.

Now do this meditation: Sit with the magazine pages spread before you, and close your eyes. Find your breath and relax in your breath for at least five minutes saying to yourself: *I am here now* (on the in breath); *I am here now* (on the out breath). Then open your eyes and as quickly as possible, *without thinking,* cut or tear out words that draw your attention. It is important that you quickly cut or tear out the words that draw your attention without thinking about them. You should not be reading or resting attention on any of the pages. Give yourself five minutes for cutting and tearing.

Now spend at least ten minutes pasting the words on another quarter of your mandala. Try not to think too much about arranging them, just pick up a word and paste it in the first place your hands move to.

Third Mandala Exercise

Give yourself about fifteen to twenty minutes in nature. While there, notice what smells, sounds, and sights draw your attention. After about ten minutes of noticing what gets your attention, begin to collect some natural objects—anything that represents natural beauty to you. Take the time to choose what attracts you, what calls your attention. These objects might include leaves, bark, seeds, flower petals, stems, a feather, twigs, or hair. Give yourself at least fifteen minutes to collect these beauty objects and then another fifteen to fill up another quarter of your mandala with them.

Fourth Mandala Exercise

Fill in the last quarter of the mandala with a poem of yours. Refer to chapter 2 for more on writing poetry.

Now write the date on the back of your mandala. Step back and look at it. Notice how beautiful and complete it is. How does it feel to have created a personal mandala?

* Meditate on your mandala. Sit quietly while holding a soft focus on it.
* With your mandala in mind, write about beauty.
* Write about wholeness.

"The streams running through my woods carry the dreams of the animals that drink here. Their dreams make the water taste sweet."

—FROM *BEAUTY AND THE BEAST* RETOLD BY NANCY WILLARD

Knowing Your True Nature through Writing

Off the Page

For more on mandalas check out Susanne F. Fincher's *Creating Mandalas for Insight, Healing and Self-Expression* and *Coloring Mandalas*, a coloring book of forty-eight sacred circle designs for people of all ages. One of the mandalas is blank (and easy to copy onto card stock). *Creating Mandalas* has a great introduction to help you get more insight into the value of personalizing mandalas.

I don't know where
such certainty comes from—
the brave flesh
or the theater of the mind—
but if I had to guess
I would say that only
what the soul is supposed to be
could send us forth
with such cheer.

—MARY OLIVER, AMERICAN POET

5

Travel Notes: Road-Trip Journaling

by Seth Taylor

The winding river
Never asks, "Where shall I turn?"
The sea waits ahead.

No greening willow
Weeps, "How is it I must stay?"
Winds send forth her seed.

The migrating crane
Does not puzzle, "Why this way?"
The way is that way.

—**D. W. ROZELLE**, POET

"As long as I live, I'll hear waterfalls and birds and winds sing. I'll interpret the rocks, learn the language of flood, storm and the avalanche. I'll acquaint myself with the glaciers and wild gardens, and get as near to the heart of the world as I can."

"Only by going alone in silence, without baggage, can one truly get into the heart of the wilderness. All other travel is mere dust and hotels and baggage and chatter."

"The world's big, and I want to have a good look at it before it gets dark."

—FROM *THE MOUNTAINS OF CALIFORNIA* BY JOHN MUIR,
NATURALIST, AUTHOR, ENVIRONMENTAL ACTIVIST

This chapter was written by my friend Seth Taylor. He has journaled since the age of ten, traveled extensively, and is presently living in China, where he writes in his journals daily. Seth is thirty-two years old.

The Greatest Stories Never Told

The trip journal is rough around the edges, scuffed, bent, stained, warped, and rippled. It's best to tie a bit of string around a retired trip journal, as the pages have a nasty habit of falling out. Sometimes, depending on the origins of the stains, strange odors waft out upon opening them. Next to the shiny covers and unbroken spines of its less well traveled companions on the shelf, the trip journal with its frayed cover and well-worn pages can appear at first to be a bit of an embarrassment. Like wandering saints and poets they may be dusty, humble creatures, but inside they are alive with the magic one can only find by moving through the world with eyes and heart open. In the end, long after you've unpacked and gone back to family and friends, your journal becomes a journey in itself. Even after many years, you will find when you pick up a travel journal that your hands still remember the textures the road has engraved upon its surface. In its pages your journey will still be alive, ready for you to return to.

Are some journeys meant not to be recorded? Certainly some of the greatest journeys of history have not been. In 1997, after a record runoff, the Kenniwick river in Washington uncovered the bones of a man. At first, archeologists assumed this was the skeleton of one of the first pioneers to the region because many of the features of the skull were Caucasian. They guessed it would be about 125 to 150 years old. When their tests came back, they could hardly believe the results. Kenniwick Man, as he is now called, was not 150 years old or 1,000 years old. Kenniwick Man was more than 9,000 years old. Unfortunately, scientists have not been able to complete their studies of the Kenniwick Man. For the moment though, their best guess is that he migrated from Europe or Central Asia to North America some 9000 years ago.

Eventually when scientists are allowed to examine and fully test the skeleton of the Kenniwick Man, we may learn even more amazing things about him. Scientists will be able to know things about his diet and may be able to perform a DNA test that will help them to pinpoint his origin more exactly. But there are many things we will never know. All but the most basic facts about him have disappeared, and all that his adventures could have taught has also disappeared. We may find out where the Kenniwick Man came from, but we will never understand why he came in the first place.

The most famous traveler of all, Marco Polo, did not intend to set the records of his travels down. Were it not for the fact that he was imprisoned with a curious scribe as the result of a failed military campaign, his story, like so many others, would have been lost forever.

Journeys without journals have their place—but it is an uncertain one. Without a physical presence of their own, memories fade away like dreams. Mere memory warps and distorts the past, remaking it to match the truths of the present. Memories have no abiding tangible presence. They can't be touched. You can't flip open a memory and

Travel Notes

run your hand over the moments as they happened. While I can't actually feel India's monsoon rains against my face when I open my journal, I can feel the patterns those raindrops made upon the pages. In this way a journal reaches across time and through the many phases of life. It's an honest testament to the way things were and the way you were when they happened.

* Write a page from the Kenniwick Man's travel journal. Where was he from? Why was he wandering around in the Pacific Northwest? Where was he going?
* Who would you most like to read your trip journal? Who do you think would learn the most from reading about your experiences?

Jumpin' Out! Travel Journals and Lessons

It is inevitable that you will learn and change while you travel. But it is impossible even to guess just what will happen or what it will mean to you. The adventures you have and the lessons they teach you are tremendous gifts. Not only will you find that you get the chance to experience new things as you travel, but at times it will feel like you have become an entirely new person.

Jumping out into the world takes faith and courage. But coming back home can be just as difficult, if not more so. In this transition it is easy to hide away or forget the truths you have found while out wandering. A journal can hold these things for you while you readjust to "normal" life. Once the readjustment is over, you can take your journal out, relive your travels, and begin to integrate what happened then and there with what is happening here and now.

The true test of a traveler is not what she can do or how far she can go. The true test of a traveler lies in what she takes out into the world to share with the people she meets there and what she brings back to touch the lives of her friends, family, and community at home.

This is the important difference between being a tourist and being a traveler. The tourist goes out to count the numbers of cities or museums or cafes that can be "done" in a week or ten days. A tourist floats above the world he travels through. When the tourist returns, he has given nothing to the people whose lives he touched in his travels, nor has he brought anything of substance or meaning back to share with the people at home. The traveler goes out to communicate with the heart of the world and returns with a part of that precious mystery to share. In short, a tourist pays extra to insulate himself from the transformational beauty of the world, while the true traveler seeks out this beauty and in turn is embraced by it.

When you get back, your journal can serve as material for talks or articles about your travels. It may also be something to share with the people close to you so they will be able to see into your thoughts. Through your writing they'll be able to experience some of the journey firsthand. You'll find people will be a lot more interested in talking with you about your travels if they have read something about your trip. By reading your story they can put themselves in your place. In a sense, your travels become a part of their lives too.

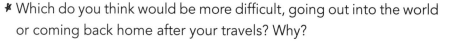

* Which do you think would be more difficult, going out into the world or coming back home after your travels? Why?
* Who would you share your journal with?
* What other things could you do with the material from your trip journal? List some of the things you could do within your community using your travel journal as a reference.
* Write about meeting a stranger.

Making Your Travel Journal Indispensable

There are no real rules for choosing a trip journal. A rolled up stack of copy paper and a rubber band might work in a pinch, as might a fancy journal from the stationery store. Both have advantages and limitations. When choosing or making a trip journal, I lean toward

"The World is a book, and those who do not travel read only a page."

—SAINT AUGUSTINE (354–430 C.E.), NORTH AFRICAN BISHOP AND PHILOSOPHER

sturdy, hardbound, unlined volumes. I make sure my journal will fit into my shoulder bag and is light enough to carry comfortably. If you have to pack your journal at the bottom of your backpack at the beginning of your journey, chances are that's where you'll find it, unmarked and unused, when you unpack at the end of the trip.

The more essential your trip journal is to your travels, the more likely it will catch your poetry as well. Trip journals are fantastic places for organizing everything from what you will bring along to what you will need to do before you leave. They can help sort out the mess of putting together what you need for any trip, particularly one that requires passports, airplane tickets, travel agents, or reservations. Stick in anything else that might come in handy along the way, from bus schedules to a record of when you began taking your malaria medication. A journal's pages are good places to jot down the friendly advice of other travelers or thoughts and quotes you would like to think on while you travel. Every one of my journeys has begun as a note in the margins of a journal. For me, the journal is where the journey truly begins.

Another advantage of recording even the most mundane details in your journal is that you will then have a single resource of travel information when you need to find something in a hurry. It can be vital to have the information you gathered at the beginning of your trip with you in some form while you are actually out wandering around. Simply being able to give the name of the person who took your reservation or quoted you a price can save you expensive and frustrating last-minute negotiations. You never know when you might need the name of that helpful ambassador's aide at the Peruvian embassy or the name of your hotel in Madras. If that particular piece of information is stuck to the back of a shoebox in the third desk drawer on the right in your room at home, it won't do you much good. By jotting down your important addresses and sundry information in a journal, you make it an indispensable tool for traveling. Every stop along the way, you'll be fishing out your journal to check a fact or remember an address. The thing about the empty pages in a journal is that, if they are close by and you have to look at them a lot, they won't stay empty for long.

* Before your next trip, take the last four or five pages in your current journal and fill them with important addresses and dates. (If you don't have plans for a real trip, invent one.)
* Can you think of any other ways to make your journal a practical partner while you travel?
* How do you cope with having too much to write all at one time? What would your advice be to another journaler?

On the Road

So once you have shouldered your bags and set off, what do you write about? It is easy to get swamped by the sheer volume of thoughts and experiences that get crammed into every minute of traveling. In such a state of sensory overload it can be difficult to pick out what to write about. Of the millions of things that surround you, which is really the one that will best help you express some of the thoughts and feelings within you? Consider that when things are really happening, you often don't have time to haul out your journal to note everything down. Afterward, it can be difficult to figure out where to begin.

So how do you do it? I find much of the adrenalin I expend traveling is spent rushing to get places, only to wait for half a day. After charging down the streets of Bangkok with a fifty-pound pack, dodging taxis and motorbikes, you may find you have to wait on the bus for two hours while the drivers search for enough passengers to fill the empty seats. These are perfect times to catch up on your journaling—but, more often than not, these are also the times when writer's block sets in.

When in doubt, start with concrete facts. Pick something, anything, that has caught your eye and describe it. As you work your way around that thing or event you will find your writing muse will have opened other doors for you. Where you begin writing, how you begin

"It's fascinating to travel around Italy and realize just how many different ways they make spaghetti."
—MARIO BATALI, CHEF, TELEVISION PERSONALITY

Travel Notes

writing, and what you begin writing about are not terribly important. That you begin in the first place is the most important thing. Don't forget, even the mundane details are going to be interesting when you reread your journal back home. In fact, it is often these very details that form the scaffolding upon which to reconstruct memories of your trip with great clarity. In terms of the actual act of writing, starting with the facts is a good way to organize your thoughts. Once you start describing what exactly you have just seen or done, you will begin to throw in thoughts, opinions, and observations naturally.

Don't be afraid of tangents or themes that seem to repeat themselves. If you have a thought or an idea, keep chasing it. Trip journals are supposed to ramble. They follow their own rules. You may have to pursue some odd directions in your writing to get to what you want to say. If you are in a completely strange place, doing things you have never done before, your creative process will naturally take some amusing and unexpected twists and turns. In travel journaling as in traveling itself, it is best to relax, keep your eyes and heart open to whatever may happen next, and enjoy the ride.

Another trick to good trip journaling is to have one consistent time and place when you will definitely write. When I travel I keep my journal by my bed (or whatever surface I happen to be sleeping on that night) so I can write down the events and thoughts of the day before I go to sleep. When I wake up, I can write down my dreams. This trick also works well to capture the sudden flashes of inspiration that happen just as you drift off to sleep and just before you are fully awake in the morning. Besides, journals can be pretty good mosquito swatters when nothing else is at hand.

❖

* Think of one thing from your day today (it could be anything) and describe it. Try to make whatever it is as clear as possible.
* Keep your journal by your bed. What is the first thing you think of when you wake up in the morning? Try to catch one thought before you fall asleep at night.
* Take a bus ride and write about what and who you see on the bus.

Speaking Their Language

Journals are also good for exploring languages. As I travel around I like to collect phrases from the people I meet along the way. Even if you will be in a place only a week or two, you can still learn enough of the language to have some fun. Phrase books are nice, but I find I remember words and phrases better when I sit down with a new friend and we make a phrase book together. Of course this can often lead to the next best thing to communicating in a foreign language—*miscommunicating* in a foreign language!

I once spent a week traveling over the Tibetan Plateau with a Tibetan phrase book I had made with a truck driver on my ride into the Himalayas. The truck driver and I had a good time trying to think of things I might need to know how to say. Since we didn't share much in terms of a mutual language, we pantomimed the meanings back and forth to each other. When he finally dropped me at a truck stop, I had four pages of crazily scribbled Tibetan along with what I had guessed to be the closest English approximations for each phrase's meaning.

The next morning I set out for the mountains. Each time I came across an encampment I called out "Thu chi-che" as a greeting. The Tibetans all smiled broadly and waved. Most of the people I ran into invited me into their tents for tea. As they poured the tea I would try my hand at saying "thank-you" by saying "tashi-delek." Again the Tibetans smiled and nodded. It wasn't until a week later when I bumped into another group of travelers who had a regular store-bought phrase book that I found that on the bumpy truck ride into the mountains I had transposed *hello* and *thank-you*. For that entire week every time I had seen a Tibetan, I had thanked them for being there. Each time I had gotten another cup of tea, I'd greeted it like an old friend, "Hello, tea!"

Every person I ran into that week smiled, and at each stop we had a lot of fun playing around and figuring out ways to communicate. But the travelers I ran into who had dutifully used their store-bought

"One of the gifts of being a writer is that it gives you an excuse to do things, to go places and explore. Another is that writing motivates you to look closely at life as it lurches by and tramps around."

—ANNE LAMOTT,
AMERICAN AUTHOR

Travel Notes

phrase book had had a lot less fun. They reported the Tibetans had been cold and not very welcoming, completely the opposite of my experience! Was my warm welcome due to the fact my phrase book had a few misplaced words? Maybe. It is impossible to tell for sure. I can tell you one thing: after studying Tibetan for six months in Dharamsala, my Tibetan is a lot better now—but I still say "Tashi Delek" to every cup of tea I get.

* Speaking a foreign language can be embarrassing. How would you get over the fear of making mistakes in a new language?
* If you had to write a phrase book for someone else in your own language, what phrases do you think would be useful?

Off the Page

Go to the library and find a phrase book on a language that you have never heard before. Copy some useful phrases into your journal. You never know when a couple of phrases of Tagalog or Urdu might come in handy.

The Many Hands and Faces of the Journey

You don't have to be the sole author of your travel journal. If you keep it nearby and are not shy, your journal will mirror your journey. Each spare moment is a chance for your journal to catch a bit of magic. Empty pages are irresistible! If you give your traveling companions and the people you meet along the way the opportunity to leave their thoughts on your pages, you might be amazed at what you find. Sometimes what we write in a journal doesn't take on its full meaning until someone else lends his or her own thoughts or images. A journal is sort of like a camera: use it to capture everything you can, but if you want a clear picture of yourself in a place it is best to hand it over to another person to operate the shutter for a while. Some of your most cherished pages may not even be filled by your own hand but by that of a stranger who passed a few hours sharing a table, a beach, or a ride with you.

Along with preserving your memories and experiences, trip journals can help you keep in touch with the people you cross paths with. They protect the thin filaments of contact information that link us to those we meet along the way. When one meditates upon the near impossibility of meeting one specific person on the road for the first time, it is tempting to think finding them again would be just as effortless. It is difficult to imagine just how lost one person can become to you in this wide world. Sure, chance meetings do happen. I have bumped into high-school friends in subway cars racing through Taipei and acquaintances from home in the back alleys of India. But having a phone number or an address means the universe doesn't have to work so hard to put the two of you back together again.

As you travel you will probably meet a lot of local people. It is surprising how much sending a photograph or two back to them after your trip can mean. If someone is kind to you on your travels and opens their door to you, send them a picture or two. If you do, you make sure that their door will remain open, not only to you but to other travelers in need. Sometimes, this is easier said than done. Often local addresses, in Asia in particular, can be nearly impossible to write. If you try to transliterate the address in English, you run the risk of sending your letter to the wrong person, the wrong town, or the wrong country altogether. The most reliable way to address an envelope is to have your friend write the address in your journal. Then when you return home you can run off a copy, add enough English to get the letter out of the United States, and the rest of the magic will happen a lot more reliably.

"Too many of us are hung up on what we don't have, can't have, or won't ever have. We spend too much energy being down, when we could use that same energy doing, or at least trying to do, some of the things we really want to do."

—TERRY McMILLAN, AMERICAN MUSICIAN

Travel Notes

- ✷ Invite someone to write a page in your journal.
- ✷ If you met someone out in the world while you were traveling and knew only the person's name and the country he or she lived in, how would you go about finding that person again?
- ✷ Write about a place you have never been to.

The Magic of Travel

There are a million reasons not to travel. It's dangerous. You never know what might happen. Even the best-planned tour has the potential to change your life in unexpected ways. Once you step out of your everyday routine, you exit the well-known corridors of life as you know it and enter the in-between spaces. This is no small thing. Most of our lives are defined by where we are and where we have to be. The world sees us, and sometimes we even see ourselves, in terms of numbers on cards and computer screens. If we are not careful we can slip into thinking of ourselves as a name, a place in a seating chart, a number on a library card, a seat on the bus, a spot on a roll call. When you step out into the world, you lose all that. Your minutes become your own, and for a while you can look wherever you would like to look and be wherever you'd like to be whenever you would like to be there. When you travel you have no history; the only thing you have to worry about is the ever-present now.

The journey is a sacred space where we get to actually touch the fabric of things. We get a chance to step behind life's stage and see how things operate. Once you travel, you will never again think of yourself or your home in the same way. While you are outside the everyday world looking in, things inevitably begin to look a little strange. By giving yourself a chance to look at the world in a new way, you get to look at your own life from a new point of view as well.

In a trip journal, you can often begin to appreciate the miraculous connections between things. Most of the people you meet while rambling through the world come into your life as the result of an amazing string of improbable circumstances. Each one is evidence of the quiet conversation between your life and the universe around you. These things are easy to miss when simply thinking back over things. Somehow, when you read the story written on the page, they stand out more clearly. How it is that any two people come to be in the same place at the same time is amazing—but it never seems quite as amazing as when it occurs in a story that takes place thousands of miles away from home.

In all of this, the trip journal plays a quiet but essential role. Traveling can be confusing and difficult and, on occasion, dangerous. When you are traveling you are often completely focused on what is happening at the moment. It is easy to miss the bigger themes and lessons. When I reread my trip journals, I sometimes find myself amazed that any of it ever happened in the first place. If there is one reason I sometimes hesitate to let people read my journals, it is because a lot of what happens in them is too far-fetched. I doubt that they would believe half of what is written there. Once I am safe at home again and life has slowed down to its normal pace, the stories my journals tell seem like fantasy; but while they were happening they were just life. Journals are one of the best tools to help you understand your journey.

People usually spend their time as they prepare for a trip imagining the things they might need. In the end, traveling always surprises you. Half the things you bring you never use, and half the things you need along the way you find you have left behind. These days when I pack bags, I try not to worry too much about what might happen. I know things will work out in their own way. What I concentrate on most is packing things that will help me grow and learn. It's even better when they help me save a record of that growth and learning for later reference. I can't think of a better traveling companion to have than a blank book with a pen clipped to the cover.

"As you think, you travel, and as you love, you attract. You are today where your thoughts have brought you; you will be tomorrow where your thoughts take you."

—JAMES LANE ALLEN, EARLY 20TH-CENTURY AMERICAN NOVELIST

Travel Notes

* Write down the top three trips you would like to take. Why do these places fascinate you? What would you do there?
* Imagine you could not only travel anywhere you'd like but also "any-when." Where and when would you go and why?
* What was the most amazing "coincidence" that ever happened to you?
* Write about a close call.

The Trip Back

Returning home is usually a lot more difficult than leaving in the first place. It is difficult to fit back in. With all that newly discovered territory in your heart and head, it can be hard to reconnect with your home. Once you begin traveling, some part of you will forever remain a foreigner. Once you reconcile yourself to this feeling, it isn't such a bad thing. But the road to integrating your travels with your life back home is not always an easy one. In fact, it may be the most difficult journey of all.

In the Greek myth of Theseus and the Minotaur, Theseus emerged from the labyrinth (the Minotaur's lair) victorious for two reasons. The first reason was that Theseus was a strong and cunning warrior (of course that's usually part of the package if you are the son of a god). The second (and I believe the more important of the two) was a gift from his love, Ariadne: a simple ball of thread.

In the myth, Ariadne was the daughter of King Minos of Crete, who had built the labyrinth in the first place. She knew the dangers of the labyrinth better than most, and she knew that, though the Minotaur was dangerous, the real danger was in getting back out again. Theseus could wander into the labyrinth, kill the Minotaur, and then never be able to find his way out again. So of all the things she could have given Theseus, she gave him a spool of thread. By tying one end of the thread to a post at the entrance of the labyrinth and paying it out behind him as he moved through the maze, he would be able to find his way out of the labyrinth after dealing with the Minotaur.

I really admire Ariadne's thinking on this one. Some friends might have given Theseus a sword or a cloak of invisibility, a bottle of water or perhaps a handful of power bars. But Ariadne believed in Theseus so much she knew he would succeed, and the only thing he'd need would be the means to find his way back to where he started. This is the spiritual task of the trip journal, too. It won't protect you from getting sick, won't stop you from losing your money or getting in an argument with your less reliable traveling companions. It won't make a taxi driver think twice before charging you more than she should to take you in a direction you don't want to go. A trip journal is worthless as a weapon, terrible as a meal, and doesn't last long as a bonfire. What does a trip journal do that is so awfully important? It gives you both a way back to where you began and a measurement of how far you have gone.

The person you are while traveling and the person you are at home are different. The longer you travel, the greater this difference becomes. This makes coming home confusing. Things and people you have known for years are so familiar, and yet strangely not. Coming back home is like returning from the center of the labyrinth. It helps to be able to read back over where you've been and how you got there when you're trying to figure out how to integrate it all into your life at home.

Once you are back, your journal becomes something Ariadne's ball of thread could never become: it becomes a journey in and of itself. Trip journals are patient creatures. They live on shelves or stuffed in boxes for years, even decades. As the journeys pile up in your life and new volumes are added to your collection, the earliest journals will wait quietly until you happen to open them up again. Then they become a portal back, not just to where you were but to who you were. They are a measuring post by which you can figure the person you have become.

"Do not ask what the world needs; ask yourself what makes you come alive. And then go and do that. Because what the world needs are people who have come alive."

—HAROLD WHITMAN, INSPIRATIONAL SPEAKER

* Have you ever gone somewhere only to return and find that you look at things a little differently at home? What happened and how do you think your experience changed you?
* After all of your travels and adventures, who is the person who would be most likely to understand you and why?
* What is your ball of thread?
* Write about getting lost.

Is It Really Necessary to Travel?

Virtually every culture in the world has woven travel into the process of personal development. Whether it is going away to university or making the pilgrimage to Mecca, going into the Peace Corps or wandering off into the Outback on walkabout, each culture embraces travel in its own way. But do you really have to leave home to travel? Do you really have to get on a plane or a train or take the car on the highway?

Traveling is really just stepping outside of your routine, your life that has already been dictated by somebody else. At its heart a journey is about stepping into the spaces between the predictable worlds we make for ourselves. It is about going out and making it back with something that changes the way you look at the everyday world. In this sense one may travel broadly in one's own backyard. A trip journal fits as well in a schoolbag, briefcase, or file folder as it does in a backpack. A journey is not the miles on the odometer or the stamps on a passport—it is about the mileage you put on your heart and the sights you have experienced in your soul.

The core of traveling is not where you go but how you go. You can "travel" wherever you are no matter how long you've been there or how long you stay. In a sense every journal is a trip journal. Every journal traces your path through life. Each one celebrates the unique adventure and the unique set of guides and lessons that create your life's journey.

Whether your travels take you to the end of the street or to the ends of the Earth, once you return home, journals keep your travels alive. What a specific trip means to you will change over time as you continue to travel and as your life continues to change and develop. With a good trip journal on your shelf, the trip itself is just the beginning. Your journal is a passage back. Through it you will be able to relive your travels and mark the changes and lessons as they happened. Some lessons take years to finally sift out from between the wrinkled pages of a trusted journal. It is amazing how our lessons can hide in a journal for years waiting for us to be ready to learn them.

In the end traveling is never about the distance you travel in the world but the distance you travel in yourself.

I graduated today—I'm done with high school and off to a new part of my life.

I think it will be good for me to start off with this trip. I am forcing myself to branch away to see new things, a different part of this amazing world we live in.

I'm a bit scared about being on my own in a foreign country and traveling home alone. But someday I will need to do it, right? So why not start now. . . .

—AMANDA, AGE 18

✦

* Imagine a traveler from a foreign country is coming to visit your hometown. Become that traveler and write a page or two of his or her trip journal.
* Write about where you are going.

Off the Page

Take a look at a map and find a place near you where you have never been before. Take a quick trip there and bring your journal along.

"If it is to be,
It is up to me."

—ANONYMOUS

6

Nature's Peace: Finding the Self through Nature

"You don't need tickets
To listen to crickets."
—FROM *INSECTLOPEDIA* BY DOUGLAS FLORIAN,
CHILDREN'S AUTHOR AND ILLUSTRATOR

"Climb the mountains and get their good tidings.
Nature's peace will flow into you
as sunshine flows into trees.
The winds will blow their own freshness into you
and the storms their energy,
While cares will drop off
like autumn falling leaves."
—JOHN MUIR, AMERICAN NATURALIST, ENVIRONMENTALIST

> "If I knew all there is to know about a golden Arctic poppy growing on a rocky ledge in the Far North, I would know the whole story of evolution and creation."
>
> —SIGURD F. OLSON, AUTHOR, NATURALIST

Meet Mother Willow

When we hang out with nature something great in ourselves wakes up. We quickly feel more complete, strong, balanced, and beautiful. Nature in all her forms becomes an ally. She waits outside your door, ready at any moment to guide you safely home to all that is true and good about yourself.

According to the legends and ancient knowledge of trees, willows represent woman's strength. The ancient Celts knew the willow as the Tree of Enchantment and Mysteries. Sitting with a willow can increase your intuitive powers, help you remember your dreams, and give you feminine strength. Feminine qualities are considered the "yin" qualities in Taoism, those qualities that are receptive. Even young men need feminine qualities, just as young women need masculine qualities. Abiding with this particular tree will get you in touch with your own deep wisdom, because this tree is also associated with creativity, visions, and poetic abilities.

> "This process of attunement with Nature I found to be very revealing, for often the trees would seem to know me better than I knew myself."
>
> —FROM *TREE WISDOM: THE DEFINITIVE GUIDEBOOK* BY JACQUELINE MEMORY PATERSON

I can be so absent minded, it seems my head is not even part of my body. I'm anxious so much of the time. I can't even remember all the things I need to get done. I shared this with my therapist and she told me to go find a willow tree to sit under, to visit, and to water. She asked that I not think too much about it, and just give it a try. She invited me to take my journal with me to write in. It just so happens I knew right where a big willow tree sits in a friend's yard, near a lake. I came to the tree with a bottle of water. I sat under her and leaned my body against hers. I instantly felt the tree's strength. Then her strength became my strength. Later, I almost fell asleep until a crow cawed at me. I felt surrounded by signs. I don't even know what they all mean, except I felt God talking to me. I have never felt this in church. I've returned several times to sit with this willow tree and give her water.

—ANNA, AGE 19

You may want to read more about tree wisdom and choose other trees to sit under and write. A great book for this is *The Wisdom of Trees: Mysteries, Magic, and Medicine* by Jane Gifford.

Consider sitting with and journaling under these trees of wisdom:

Apple The apple tree is a tree of wisdom and healing. Many seek the medicinal powers of its fruit, flowers, and bark. Sit with the apple tree when you are seeking insight on how to heal. You may also receive poetic inspiration under the apple tree.

Beech The beech tree is a writer's tree. Jane Gifford used this tree to glean some wisdom for her book. She tells us the beech "is a symbol for the written word and for the innate wisdom contained within it, and for ancient learning." Sit under this great tree to consult oracles (see pages 59–61) for it helps you contact ancient wisdom.

Rowan The rowan tree (also known as mountain ash) is known for its ability to offer spiritual strength and awaken us to our place in the circle of life. If you feel alone and disconnected from the world, sit with a rowan.

Alder The alder tree is a masculine tree that holds protective energies and strengthens our inner confidence. Legend tells us that this tree is also considered a fairy tree—a good place to feel your own magic.

Hawthorn The hawthorn tree can strengthen the emotions of the heart, and open up your heart to love (in all the forms it takes). It can be a blessing tree for a love relationship. This would be a good tree to visit with a loved one, or to marry under.

Oak The oak tree's energies will help you endure and give you strength. Oak is a masculine tree. Write and say a prayer under this tree. This tree is also known for its gifts of prophecy, so under an oak is another good place to consult an oracle.

* Imagine yourself as a tree. What tree would it be? Write about that.
* Write about going out on a limb.
* Write about an apple falling very far from the tree.

Off the Page

Give yourself a couple of hours. Find a nearby willow tree that you can sit with for at least half an hour. Take your journal with you, and some water for you and the tree. (The water is for thanking the tree.)

First sit with the tree as Anna did. Then listen and notice how you feel on the inside as you let her energy mingle with yours. What do you notice? Write this down. Notice any wildlife, a leaf falling to the ground, sounds and smells that present themselves while you sit there. Abide with the tree for a while, just noticing, before you begin to write.

When you are done journaling, and before leaving, thank the tree for its wisdom and offer her some water.

The Everyday Divine

Who bends a knee where violets grow
A hundred secret things shall know.

—RACHEL FIELD, AMERICAN AUTHOR AND POET

Each of us can uncover the divine (God, Spirit, the Tao) in nature; we simply need to notice that she is actually interacting with us. I tune in to the radio on my commute from work. Once, I listened

"The central root of a tree is called the taproot. Besides providing the tree with nourishment, this taproot is the tree's main 'anchor.' What is your main anchor? What gives you a sense of stability and a sense of 'rootedness'?"

—FROM *A NEW LEAF: IDEAS FOR WRITING INSPIRED BY TREES* BY M. S. D. SAMSTON

"Listen to the voice of nature, for it holds treasures for you."

—HURON PROVERB

to a station where people call in with their problems and the host offers some religious advice and a song. The producer of the show shared a story of how the house she lives in is being tapped by woodpeckers. The previous owner was not bothered by woodpeckers. In fact, the host has had all sorts of animals showing up in her house, including a family of raccoons. None of this happened with the previous owner. The host opened up this "problem" of the woodpeckers to the listening public.

One listener called in and related that he and his wife lived in a home where for the past six years a woodpecker woke them every day with his insistent tapping. The house was being damaged. Because the woodpecker is a protected species, they could not harm it in any way. They tried everything to get the bird to leave their house alone. Finally, the couple moved across town. Shortly after they were all unpacked, the sound of the woodpecker on their new home awakened them! They called and asked the present owners of their last home if there was a woodpecker chipping away at the house in the mornings. "No," they replied, "we haven't had any problems or sign of a woodpecker."

What might be happening here?

I wanted to call the station to suggest that this couple consider the possibility that the woodpecker was trying to tell them something! As Jeremiah, a twenty-one-year-old college student of religious studies, writes: "If it is true that God is everywhere and in everything, doesn't it make sense that the woodpecker could be a messenger?"

I looked up woodpecker in Jessica Dawn Palmer's *Animal Wisdom.* This is what she writes: "The woodpecker is associated with storms, thunder, trees and tree magic, sacred circles and mother earth. It represents air, fire, water and earth, and as such woodpecker medicine is good 'all-round' medicine to have." It pecks at us to remind us to get in touch with Mother Earth's cycles. Palmer also warns that "woodpecker can . . . bode that the individual is out of sync or out of step (in their life or with mother nature). Whenever woodpecker arrives it is time to listen." Is Mother Earth trying to get these people's attention? Are they listening?

* Write down what you think the woodpecker may be trying to say, or why the woodpecker seemed to follow this couple to their new home.
* Notice which animals may appear routinely in your life. First write about the encounters with these animals, when and how they appear. Then, write what a particular animal or insect means to you. For example, what does a snake mean to you? What does a tree frog mean to you? What might the sound of a crow cawing outside your window every morning mean?

Off the Page

After you write your own meaning and interpretation of this meeting with nature, do some research to find out the mythical and mystical meaning of this wildlife. Now what do you think the message of the animal might be? What is this animal pointing to? What does Spirit want you to pay attention to? Record this in your journal.

The Elemental Powers: Earth, Water, Fire, Air

The four elements are inherent in every living thing. The actual presence of fire may not be in something, but the metaphysical element of fire is—for fire refers to all luminous and electrical states. Each of the four elements represents powerful principles and energies that you can tap into. The four elements are represented in the signs of the zodiac, the Native American Medicine Wheel, the I Ching, and the tarot. In Tibetan medicine, as well as other Eastern practices such as acupuncture and Tao shiatsu, each of us is seen as being either in balance with the internal four elements or out of balance.

For example, if you can "go with the flow," the element of water is strong in you. However, if others too easily influence you, perhaps you have too much water energy and need more fire or earth. Someone who speaks too much is said to have too much wind energy, or air. Ideally, these elemental powers are somewhat balanced in you, but in a particular mix that complements your uniqueness.

The qualities associated with the four elements are listed below.

The element of fire is related to creativity, intuition, sexuality, and spirit. Fire people are often creative and enthusiastic, sometimes domineering. Fire energizes. Fire is the power of transformation and dramatic change.

The element of water is related to the soul and is associated with the emotions, sensitivity, and being receptive and fluid. Water people are more easygoing and can adapt themselves to new and changing situations. Water expresses the powers of slow change, imagination, and quiet qualities.

The element of air is related to thoughts and ideas, as well as speech. It is the element of communication. It can represent psychic communication. Air people can become easily bored so need to be involved in something all the time. Many prolific writers have a strong air quality.

The element of earth is related to the physical body and all its sensations. It represents stability, patience, and persistence, organic qualities, and sensuality. Because of earth's abundance, earth people are often prosperous. Earth people are dependable. Earth people are grounded, stable, and centered.

✱ Write about your elemental qualities. Are you full of air, or fire? Choose one and write about yourself as this element. Repeat the sentence "I am a person of (elemental power)" without stopping to think. Let yourself be this element.

> I am a person of water when I am at school but after school I am a person of fire and air. I am a person of water at school otherwise I would burn myself up. I am a person of water. I am a person of water when I am at school. The teachers see me as this good student but inside I am fire and air, inside I am fire and air, inside I am fire and air. I am a person of water at school and my body moves down the halls past the lockers, past the seniors, past the teachers waiting, and into the classroom where I sit like a drop of water in a large pool of water. I am a person of water at school. I am a person of water at school until I get out and my fire and air come out. Then, I am a person of fire and air.
>
> —ADLEY, AGE 16

* Read up on your astrological sign. What element is prevalent in your sign? Write about this. A good resource for this is *Teen Astrology* by M. J. Abadie.
* Write about going with the flow.
* Write about setting yourself on fire (metaphorically).
* Write about being an airhead.
* Write about being grounded.

The Mother Knows

> "Let us join the Great Mother,
> Change blood into milk, clay into vessel,
> egg into child, wind into song,
> our bodies into worship."
>
> —ELIZABETH ROBERTS, ARTIST

All original cultures—Native Americans, Celts, Australian aborigines, African tribes, the desert peoples—know that the Earth *is* our

"In God's wildness is the hope of the world—the great fresh, unblighted, unredeemed wilderness."

—JOHN MUIR

Nature's Peace

mother. We depend on her for our very life. So how is it we are moving so far away from her? Elders from many Native American tribes, as well as other present day wisdomkeepers (Eckhart Tolle, Ram Das, Lama Surya Das), know that our time is limited on this Earth if we persist in the way we are going now. It is not so much that the Earth will be destroyed, it is more likely that she will spit us out like a body spits out a disease. Global warming, for example, can be likened to a high body temperature, or fever. This heat helps expel the disease from the body—whatever is causing the temperature to rise. Mother Earth is powerful. She does not like to be ignored or mistreated. We cannot escape the reality that our very lives depend on how we care for her. As you know, global warming in reality results in a variety of problematic weather changes, not just increasing temperatures.

For me, the Earth is a breathing being with a soul so big it took a planet to hold it. Everything I do as I walk on her body affects her and everyone else on the planet. I know I can walk on her more carefully. Each day as part of my prayer I ask myself, What can I do for Mother Earth today? Then, as part of my morning ritual I honor the Earth Mother by pouring a bowl of water into her and thanking her. Some elders warn us that Mother Earth, the soul of the Earth, is in so much pain she is thinking of leaving. This feels true to me, and so I pour the water, and ask the question "What can I do for you today?" Some days this might mean reusing a water bottle rather than buying a new one every time I am thirsty. On other days it might mean picking up someone else's litter lying by the side of the road.

✶ What can you do for the Earth today? Write it down in your journal as a reminder.
✶ Write about a time (real or imagined) you got lost in the woods.
✶ Write about a time you felt connected to Mother Earth.
✶ Take your journal and go outside. . . .

"Spontaneous me, Nature,
The loving day,
the mounting sun,
the friend I am happy
with . . . ."

—**WALT WHITMAN, AMERICAN POET**

Off the Page

Fill up a bowl with water and pour it into the Earth. Thank her.

Wild Life

"There was wildfire to be caught before it was tamed and kindled; there were dreams, visions arising from hunger or possibly from psychotropic mushrooms, that spoke with voices from other realms; there was dancing and singing and coupling; there was language; there was the roar of the thunder and the jagged spear of lightning hurled down to earth—by whom or what?—from the unfathomable height of the luminous sky. There were the wheeling stars at night and the great warmth of the sun that vanquished the stars at dawn."

—FROM *THE CODE OF THE WARRIOR*
BY **RICK FIELDS, AMERICAN AUTHOR**

"We had the sky, up there, all speckled with stars, and we used to lay on our backs and look up at them, and discuss about whether they was made, or only just happened."

—FROM *HUCKLEBERRY FINN* BY **MARK TWAIN**

In the excerpt above, Rick Fields is speaking of early humans in Africa. Their relationship to the natural world and to Spirit was intense and real. We need to bring this intensity back through connection to the Earth and to our true nature. Our bodies need the fresh air and all the elements to bring forth in us our own wild nature. Feeling bored and dull? Go for a brisk walk outside. Go watch the waves crash on

Nature's Peace

the shore, or gaze at the sunset after a storm. It is unnatural to be so subdued and tame—*it is in our nature to be in nature.*

There is something wild in us all. Granted, we are pretty well domesticated and tamed. Most often we are well behaved and know when to wait our turn in line. But the wildness I am talking about is there inside of you and me—wanting to come out. It needs to come out. And one of the easiest ways to invite it out is to go out and be in the wild yourself.

Off the Page

Take your journal and a pen. And if you have a camera take that, too. Find a wild prairie. Find a natural beach. Find a healthy stream or creek. Find a hillside that is preserved. Find a wild place in nature. Notice what sounds, smells, sights are around you. What is the ground like that lies beneath you? Write about all that you see, hear, smell. Give yourself an hour. Notice what changes in that hour.

Go find a place to observe the night sky outside the city limits. Lie on the ground looking up. Write about what you feel.

Field Notes

—by Al Cornell, wildlife photographer

Photos on my wall or in my album remind me of special moments when I encountered wildlife. Many of those photos originated when I managed to overcome the wary alert systems of the animal involved and had an encounter within the animal's normal flight zone. I wore camouflage or hid in a blind, so the animal did not know I was present. That made it possible for me to experience the nature of the animal in a way I could not have done from a greater distance.

Observing and photographing prairie chickens delivers a special meaning. The sight and sound of a prairie chicken *lek,* or booming ground, at the crack of dawn touches one's soul with delight and a sense of history. The strange displays of the cock birds attempting to attract hens for mating are entertaining. An air sac, like a small yellow balloon, fills up along each side of the bird's neck. The prairie chicken slowly issues an eerie, deep, resonate, "Mmm-wall-oomm." As I observe the males' posturing and then the foot-stomp display, I know I'm viewing wildlife that influenced some ceremonial dances of Native Americans. This displaying, too, touches me. If I had only observed the displaying prairie chickens, I still would have long remembered their show, but the photos I took will help me to remember details of their act and to explain it to my friends.

"If a flower blooms once, it goes on blooming somewhere forever. It blooms on for whoever has seen it blooming."

—FROM *SOUNDER* BY WILLIAM H. ARMSTRONG, AFRICAN-AMERICAN NOVELIST

Photograph of greater prairie chickens by Al Cornell

Nature's Peace

Begin your own book of field notes and photos or drawings. Local bird stores have field journals to purchase or you can simply create your own. The ones in the store are usually waterproof.

Off the Page

Take your journal and camera out to a place where you can easily observe wildlife. Hide in a blind or wear camouflage. Sit as still as possible and watch the undisturbed wildlife. Journal about their behavior as Al did in the above piece.

Take your camera and journal to a favorite spot in nature at sunrise. Take field notes and photos of what you see and hear.

Read *A Sand County Almanac* by Aldo Leopold, American naturalist and ecologist. These essays on the Round River are an example of field notes turned into a popular book.

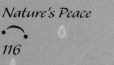

Nature's Peace

7

Inside You Is the World: Writes of Passage

"In the beginning, there is struggle and a lot of work for those who come near to God. But after that, there is indescribable joy. It is just like building a fire: at first it's smoky and your eyes water, but later you get the desired result. Thus we ought to light the Divine fire in ourselves with tears and effort."

—AMMA SYNCLETICA, EGYPTIAN HERMITESS,
WRITER, DESERT MOTHER

"I aint what I wanna be
I aint what I'm gonna be
but Oh Lord
I aint what I used to be."

—FROM AN UNKNOWN SLAVE

Inside You Is the World

"Every head is a world."

—CUBAN PROVERB

Every invention is first an idea. Every creation begins first inside someone's head. Inside your head right now is an idea, a beginning of something, a seed of creation.

Your brain is a remarkable organ. During your teen and young adult years your brain is busy developing its greatest potentials. Did you know your brain stores everything you have ever heard, studied, seen, felt, or done? Your brain is filled with ideas, questions, information, and experiences.

Take a few minutes to have a conversation with your brain.

Close your eyes and bring your attention to your breath. Just let yourself breathe naturally, and rest your attention on your breath. Then begin to give yourself permission to relax more and more on each exhalation.

Now bring your awareness to your head. . . . As you continue to breathe, imagine the intricacies of your brain, its complexities and its many functions. Imagine on each breath your brain is relaxed and open to your questions. Become aware of the power and potential of this organ. Within it is every moment of your life so far. Spend a couple of minutes visiting your brain . . . experiencing how extraordinary it is, the world of information and memories it holds. It can reveal to you any of its stored information. Imagine yourself holding a conversation with this part of you and ask it to reveal some idea it has been holding on to for you. Just breathe and ask, and trust what comes. What idea comes from it today? Let your brain visit with you. Let it talk to you.

Now turn your attention back to your breath. And when you are ready, open your eyes and journal what your brain shared with you. Repeat the line "My great idea is . . ." every time you find you want to stop writing. Keep the pen moving until you have filled the page.

* My great idea is . . .
* Write about being brainless.
* The world in my head . . .
* A place I would never want to visit . . .

Don't Give Yourself Away

If you spend too much of your time giving yourself away, later in your life you will have to invest a heck of a lot of time gathering yourself back together. So, the sooner you get good at keeping yourself together—*being* yourself—the better. Carl Jung refers to the journey toward independence and autonomy as individuation. The fact is, you must individuate in order to truly live your life. Those who do not individuate (and there are way too many who fall into this category!) live someone else's life. They live an unlived life.

So, what is individuation? It is the ability to separate yourself enough emotionally from your parents and others so that you can live the life that is truly your own. Each of us must give up the life that someone else may have in mind for us in order to live the life the Creator or our soul intends. You may have a lot of your mother's and father's genes but you are not their clone.

Throughout your teen years and early twenties you should be experiencing this individuation process. Ideally, your parents will support this transformation. Even in healthy, loving families, the individuation process can be somewhat disruptive. Chances are some of your anger and resentment (if you have any) toward your parents is one way you express your individuation—to make it abundantly clear that you are not like them. Anger is a way to separate yourself from them.

You are going to surprise your family, your neighbors, and even your friends when you take the journey that is yours to take. Your

"Choice is a divine teacher: for when we choose we learn that nothing is ever put in our path without a reason."

—Iyanla Vanzant, African-American author, inspirational speaker

Inside You Is the World

journal will be a comrade in this process, a place you can just let out what needs to get out. It can sometimes be a lifeline.

Wednesday, May 23, 2001

God, I'm trying so hard to deal gracefully with all of this, but i don't know what to do. The thing that's making it so difficult now is my hope, i think. without it I'd be packing. . . . On the phone with my mom . . .

When talking to God, you can see that you never lose What you've been fighting for. It's there. You just don't know what "it" is yet. When talking to People, sometimes you just can't help but feel you're lost. Yeah, I know it's all gonna work out somehow . . . I can accept God's plans. The hard part is carrying them out.

—LIA ELLASON, POET, AT AGE 19, TRYING TO LIVE ON HER OWN

This is a good example of a time I started writing when I felt very hopeless and lost. I was in a bad situation, living with an alcoholic boyfriend and unable to pay my rent, so I knew I'd have to be moving back in with my parents, which was difficult to accept. But I sort of found some peace of mind after writing just a short while by looking at "the bigger picture."

—LIA, AT AGE 21, NOW LIVING ON HER OWN IN HER RECENTLY PURCHASED HOME

* How's it going for you with this growing up thing so far? Write about your individuation experiences.
* What does "coming of age" mean to you—what is it we come to?
* How are your parents taking your coming of age—your growing up?
* Write about running away from home.

I can't believe this is my last week of high school forever! I am leaving on June 1st to go to Europe for twenty days! I'm very excited!

I was a bit nervous because part of the trip I will be staying by myself with a family friend of a friend in Barcelona. I know her a little bit, at least. I just was a little scared to travel on my own. But I have always wanted to travel. So if I don't start now when will I, right?

I have always loved that quote by Andre Gide in your book *Teen Psychic:*

"We can never discover new oceans if we don't have courage to lose sight of the shore." I think my trip was meant to be because for some reason the day I was trying to decide for sure what to do I came across this quote.

—and it's so very true.

I feel like sometimes I am afraid to go out and do things and I'm not entirely sure why. I think part of it is the way my mom's family is—I have grown up around them a lot. My mom doesn't always like to branch out a lot to other people and experiences. She often tries to keep me "safe" at home.

Not that I don't want to be connected with my family—because I love them. It's just I know it's good to branch out a bit too in order to broaden my views. I'm glad that my dad encourages me to go out and travel and see new places—it helps me break away from the "safety bubble."

I don't know why it was so hard for me to make a decision about traveling to a different country. It is something I have always wanted to do—but then when it was sitting right in front of me I got scared.

I know it is a good thing to step out a bit to experience new encounters, otherwise I would be going down the same path all my life without knowing anything else, seeing anything else, experiencing. My dad always told me that I could learn more traveling then I could ever learn in school.

—AMANDA, AGE 18

> "Some day you will turn around and face your parents and say, ' I am a man. I am a woman, and these are my values."
>
> —TOM BALISTRIERI,
> TEACHER OF THE
> LAKOTA TRADITIONS

* "If parents don't cut the strings, you need to." Write about this.
* List the ways you have given yourself away.
* Write about when *no* is really a *yes*.
* Write about what your parents want you to grow up to be.
* Write about who believes in you.

Inside You Is the World

The Ugly Duckling

> "For the last two centuries, 'The Ugly Duckling' has been one of the few stories to encourage successive generations of 'outsiders' to hold on till they find their own."
>
> —FROM *WOMEN WHO RUN WITH THE WOLVES*
> BY CLARISSA PINKOLA ESTÉS, PH.D.

The Ugly Duckling story holds great significance for me. Throughout my teen and young adult years I felt as if I were in the wrong family. If it is true (as some spiritual traditions claim) that we choose our family, I wondered, how did I choose this one? Frankly, I did not belong. I was the oddly shaped egg that rolled over into the wrong nest and was hatched among strangers. And just as in "The Ugly Duckling," no one in my family particularly thought I fit in. I didn't wish this upon myself, nor do I believe they wished this for me.

Fortunately, my story "ends" very much like the Ugly Duckling's—I, too, find my true family of like-minded beings outside of the one I grew up in. Living now among friends and new family, I know where I belong; I know who I am. For this to happen I had to leave the nest, and I had to choose to find others who looked and acted more like me (other swans). I chose to individuate and claim my inner independence.

> "The other important aspect of the story is that when an individual's particular kind of soulfulness, which is both an instinctual and a spiritual identity, is surrounded by psychic acknowledgment and acceptance, that person feels life and power as never before. Ascertaining one's own psychic family brings a person vitality and belongingness."
>
> —CLARISSA PINKOLA ESTÉS, PH.D.

✴ Write about leaving your nest, your family.
✴ Write about belonging.
✴ Describe your "true family."

Inside You Is the World

122

* What does Clarissa mean by "psychic acknowledgment"?
* What traits of yours do you get from your father?
* What traits of yours do you get from your mother?

Sitting on Top of the Great Mountain

Take a moment and imagine yourself on top of a great mountain. You are far above everything and can see for great distances in all directions. Use this great vision to see your life. . . .

Behind you is your life so far . . . all that has come to pass up to this moment. What do you see? What events brought you to this place in your life? What choices did you or others make that determined your life so far? How have you used this time? Can you see how one choice leads into another? What losses, trauma, or pain have you suffered? How have these affected you? What gifts, happiness, and opportunities have been given to you so far? Notice how all this has led you to YOUR LIFE NOW.

To your sides is your life now. Who are your friends? What do you give your time to? What pain are you experiencing? What gifts and opportunities are being offered to you now? What choices are you making that will determine what is to come? What are your dreams and fears? What problems and challenges face your community and the planet at this time?

In front of you is your future. What do you see? When you look in this direction it stretches out further, beyond all that you can see. But what awaits you in the near future, because of how you are living now? What do you see awaiting you and the planet in the distant future if you continue to go on as you are presently? Can you easily imagine that the future side of the mountain is vast and expansive, meaning there are many possibilities out there for you?

✦

* Write and date your responses in your journal.
* Some time in the future, repeat this meditation. Now what do you see as you sit on top of the great mountain?

"We are what we imagine. Our very existence consists in our imagination of ourselves. . . . The greatest tragedy that can befall us is to go unimagined."

—FROM *INDIAN VOICES* BY N. SCOTT MOMADAY, NATIVE AMERICAN WRITER, PULITZER PRIZE WINNER FOR FICTION

Three Travelers

Three travelers were walking down the path of life, all three with important destinations in mind. As they walked, they came upon a beautiful crystal vase that had broken. Next to the broken vase was a large rock.

The first traveler became angry and frustrated at seeing such a beautiful object in pieces. She asked, "Who did this? Did the vase hit the rock or did the rock hit the vase? Who is to blame for this?" This question caused her great anger and confusion, and she sat down next to the pile of glass trying to figure it all out.

The second traveler asked, "Why? Why did this happen? Why would God let such a thing happen to something so beautiful? Why?" And this question caused the traveler to sink into a deep state of hopelessness and helplessness and he sat unable to move, frozen in his despair.

The third traveler agreed that it was a sad thing that such a beautiful vase would meet such an end. But she did not ask "Who?" or "Why?" Instead, she said, "I am not sure who did this, who is to blame, or why this happened. I was not here. I cannot be certain. The vase is broken either way." She bent over and gently picked up the broken pieces of the vase and put them in her pocket. As she walked she made the sound of wind chimes with the glass tinkling against her moving leg.

The moral of this story is: Focus on the WHAT—what is happening and what can be done about it. Let go of the need to blame and obsessively trying to figure it out.

* What is happening in your life right now? Write about the *what*.
* Write about the fourth traveler.

> The fourth traveler was stoned on drugs and cut himself on the glass and wandered off into the woods bleeding, never to be seen again.
> —YOUNG WOMAN AT A WRITER'S WORKSHOP

> The fourth traveler didn't care. —JACK, AGE 15

* Who have you been blaming?
* Write about hopelessness.
* Write about worrying.

A World of Beliefs

Baha'i
Buddhism (Tibetan, Zen)
Christianity (Catholic, Mormon,
    Protestant, Unity, Quaker)
Confucianism
Falun Gong
Hinduism
Islam
Judaism

Jainism
Pagan and Earth-Based
Scientology
Shinto
Sikhism
Taoism
Unitarian Universalist
Zoroastrians

Amazing, isn't it? This list of sixteen religious sects is not all the world has to offer. There are the aboriginal religions of Africa, Australia, and Polynesia; the ancient spiritual traditions stemming from Celtic beliefs. There are the many tribal practices of Native Americans, and all the ancient Greek religions and philosophies. There are many types of Buddhism and Christianity. Like a wild prairie in full bloom with big bluestem, Indian grass, rattlesnake master, and purple coneflower, our globe is blooming with a multitude of spiritual traditions. Like the grasses and flowers in the prairie, the traditions share some common ground (such as some form of the Golden Rule), and they also have their differences (such as their names for God).

I am searching for religion. Two faithful Christians raised me. I have recently been inspired to research other religions, but my mother is completely convinced I will soon realize that Christianity is the "right" religion. I completely disagree. I don't believe that there is one true religion. So, I am now searching for a religion that best matches my mind and spirit. The two faiths that I have found I best relate to are Buddhism and Quakerism.

—OLIVIA, AGE 17

"You write about what you know or you write about what you want to know."

—JILL CIMENT,
AMERICAN WRITER

I can relate to wanting to look for the truth rather than have it told to you. Although it might be comforting to be told the truth and know it is the truth. But who really knows. . . . We've got to find out for ourselves. I believe in facts so I am just poring over different texts and finding what is the most altruistic.

—NOEL, AGE 19, FROM HIS ONLINE JOURNAL

* ✶ "The truth will set you free." Write about that.
* ✶ What are you looking for in a religion or spiritual practice?
* ✶ Write about being converted.
* ✶ Write about "Letting go and letting God."

Off the Page

Go to www.beliefnet.com and discover at least three unfamiliar spiritual traditions. Write about your experience.

The site also hosts a wonderful dialogue among teens. Chat with other people about your questions, your thoughts, and your search.

Inner Independence

Even if you aren't free on the outside, *you can be free on the inside.* It is not necessary to have outer independence—being free of physical or social restrictions—in order to have inner independence. In fact, most people get the two confused. They assume that because they *have to* live with their parents, or *have to* listen to their boss, or *have to* finish school, they are not truly independent. The truth is, inner independence is something that you experience no matter what is going on around you. On the outside someone you like may not be interested in you; on the outside life may be scary and painful; on the outside your older sibling may be teasing you. But on the inside *you are strong* and you can stick to what you know to be correct and true for yourself.

I compare inner independence to standing on an ocean beach where big waves are coming in. You stand there facing the ocean and the big wave hits you hard, head-on, and covers your entire body with water. This wave is any person or situation in your life that is trying to throw you off. But you hold your ground, and the wave rushes past you and back out into the ocean. You remain firmly planted in your inner truth. Someone teases you (the wave hitting you hard), but you know yourself and you refuse to get into it with this person (feet planted firmly on the ground). Then the person gives up because they are not getting you to engage in their game (the wave returns to the ocean). And you remain focused on what you know to be true (feet still firmly on the ground, facing the ocean and its magnificence).

This is inner independence. By not letting the outside world knock you off your feet, not letting another's immature or thoughtless behavior make you lose sight of your truth, you remain free—independent. Your independence comes from the inside.

* ✶ Write about being thrown off your center.
* ✶ Write about being teased.
* ✶ Write about living with your parents.
* ✶ Write about independence.

Off the Page

Make a road trip to the ocean, or get a recording of the sound of ocean waves. Meditate, listening to the waves move in and out, imagining yourself standing firm on the beach.

Inside You Is the World

Being Senior

Every time I was around her I would feel myself shrink, get small and lose what I thought I knew. How is it that when I am around certain people I shrink like one of those sponge "miracle" dolls that grow to real size in water, but quickly shrink back up when they're out of water? Is it possible to be around anyone and everyone and not shrink—to always maintain my true "size"?

—TEEN'S E-MAIL TO AUTHOR

I have a tool that I use in this kind of situation, something that was taught to me in a spiritual development class and has remained central to my inner independence ever since. I call it Being Senior.

Being a high school senior is a big deal. Seniors have "put in their time" as high schoolers, and they are recognized by teachers and younger students as special, no longer children but responsible young people on the threshold of adult life. We feel this respect and validation at the time we are seniors, and years later we remember the significance of that last year of school. Being Senior is about carrying that state of mind with you throughout your life—that knowledge that you are a valuable person who has the right to be unique and follow your own inner truth, regardless of outside circumstances.

Keeping your seniority is really about personal empowerment. Now I could just say "keep your personal power." But the word *power* has so many negative connotations that I prefer to use a new term that can help your mind open up to a new idea, and even to an entirely new way of being.

Being senior is not letting anything get bigger than you. This includes outside circumstances, the behavior of others, and your emotions. We tend to lose our seniority most often to our own emotions. Your fears and your worries often can seem a lot bigger than you. A good way to picture this is to imagine that the emotion—let's say anger—has kicked you out of the driver's seat and is now in command! Can you imagine feeling intensely about something without losing yourself, giving over your seniority to it?

There are people who instinctively understand that to get you caught up in your emotions is the way to undermine you. You can find yourself losing your seniority to them—*shrinking* around them. Being Senior means not giving *you* over to anything or anyone. It means never agreeing to shrink.

* Write about a time you felt yourself shrink around someone.
* Write about getting your seniority back.

Seniority versus Power

Throughout our lives we find ourselves in situations where others have more power than we do; sometimes they even have power over us. Certainly this is true of the teacher-student relationship. Teachers hold the power, and how they use this power can determine whether their students have a positive classroom experience or a negative one. For those times when you find yourself in the target zone of someone's misuse of power, keeping your seniority is a way to keep your soul strong and intact—to not get swallowed up in another person's power trip. You can't change the other person but you *can* choose not to feel small; not to let their power trip be bigger than you.

Letting others think what they will, as long as you are acting out of integrity, is a sure way of keeping your seniority in challenging situations. You can't change someone's way of thinking, so do instead what feels honorable to you. Base your choices and behavior on what feels right and true for you—rather than trying to get a reaction out of the other person—and you have kept your seniority.

* Write about a bad boss or teacher.
* Write about power trips.
* No one said anything but I knew that . . .
* Adults can be bullies too.

"If we had to say what writing is, we would define it essentially as an act of courage."

—CYNTHIA OZICK, AMERICAN-JEWISH AUTHOR, ESSAYIST

Inside You Is the World

The Unpaved Path

At this time in your life you will be acquiring some skills and some insights that others around you may not have. Imagine what it is like for someone in a family of alcoholics to go into recovery, to give up alcohol and drugs while everyone else in the family continues in substance abuse. Or imagine discovering you are gay in a family that opposes this lifestyle on religious grounds. Imagine being the first to go away to college from a family in which everyone else stayed in the town you grew up in. How does one do this? It is painful and at times lonely when your parents or siblings are making choices you no longer agree with or choose for yourself. It is even more difficult when you still live under their roof and depend on them.

> I can't get myself to end the relationship. I am confused and scared. We've been together for over a year and he moved in with my parents and me six months ago. He says he will kill my dog if I end our relationship. I don't think I can anyway. I might love him. He wants me to stay here and forget about going away to college. My parents like him. He threatens to kill himself if I go.
>
> And it isn't so bad. I don't know what to do. I just don't know. I think I will hang in there till I graduate (in a year) and just leave for college. Yeah, go to a place no one knows me. But hardly anyone escapes this town. I just don't know.
>
> —TERESE, AGE 16

Terese's parents do not have her best interests in mind. Perhaps they thought they were helping her out by letting her boyfriend move in, but it isn't working out that way. Too often parents make choices to please their child. But this motivation can backfire. (I asked Terese why her parents let her boyfriend move in with her when she was only fifteen. She said that they didn't want her mad at them!)

Terese will have to pave her own way. She is going to have to want her independence enough to initiate a new path. It will not be the path her parents or her boyfriend paved for her.

* Write Terese a letter. What do you think she needs to do?
* How is your path different from your parents'?
* How is your path similar to your parents'?
* Write a happy ending.
* Write a plan of escape.

Power Letters

When I open my journals from twenty or thirty years back and read what I call my "power letters" (many unsent), I feel proud of myself for speaking up. I read the emotion and intention in the letters and remember the path I was on then, and how it led to the one I am on now. I experienced some of my most empowering confrontations in my letters. Each letter reminded me of what I stood for, and what I would not stand for.

Mostly what goes into a power letter is your truth. Tell them the truth. All of it. Draw the line in the sand and feel the strength you gain by setting this boundary. Bring to the page those things you most want to express—perceptions, thoughts, feelings, and desires—but may not feel safe or sure enough to say out loud to someone.

You don't need to send the letter. It is written mostly to release the emotions and thoughts you are having about someone, and to remind yourself later about what you knew to be true for you in that relationship. If you ever feel yourself losing your seniority with this person, reread your letter.

* Pick three people with whom you have a significant relationship (parent, sibling, friend, boss, teacher, boyfriend or girlfriend, etc.) and take the time to write each of them a power letter.
* Write about boundaries.

The Demon of Self-Doubt

> "Doubt is the hoarfrost that precedes the ice of giving up."
> —From *Guide to the I Ching* by Carol K. Anthony

Hoarfrost is the bright sparkle of heavy frost that covers everything on a cold winter morning. As beautiful as it appears, it's a warning to prepare for a very cold day because ice follows the hoarfrost.

Just as the hoarfrost looks attractive, the voice of doubt can be very seductive and believable. But doubt precedes giving up on ourselves and on others. How does doubt come up for you? Where does the hoarfrost of doubt cover a plan or dream, threatening to freeze it by making you give up on something you once believed in?

Doubt puts an end to the best of ideas, plans, and intentions. Doubt is a toxin in the mind that will poison our creative intentions. Doubt, although often subtle, is powerful and needs to be confronted assertively. If we are raised in a family environment of constant criticism, we often learn to doubt our worth and ourselves. When others make too many choices for us or our parents are overly protective, we may fall into doubt when we are on our own. Doubt is not rooted in reality—it is rooted in habitual thoughts. It's a tape that is just playing over and over in your head, preventing you from trusting your intuition.

So when doubt appears in your thoughts, do your best to suspend it. Turn away from it and focus your mind on what it is you want, what it is you hope for, what your intuition tells you. Take some time to refocus through journaling.

* Write about hoarfrost.
* What part of your life may be covered in doubt?
* Write about doubting yourself only to find out *you were right* all along.
* Name your doubts. What is it exactly that you feel doubtful about?

Give Your Dreams Legs

"What are you doing with your life after high school?" It's the question every friend and relative asks once you reach your senior year.

Does this question bother you? Or does it send positive feelings throughout your body? Do you have a set answer or do you find yourself going off never really answering the question? Or do you find yourself giving your teacher's answer, or your parent's answer?

As an older adult I am often asked, "What do you *do*?" I never really know how to respond to the question about what it is I do. Perhaps we ask this question because it is more polite than coming right out and asking someone "What do you *have*?" I have a house, a car, a job. But what I *really* have is a home, places to go, and a love for people and words. And as long as I have given myself the *freedom to experience* these things, the question of what I do is somewhat moot.

Of course having some plan is important—knowing what you want and going for it is what growing up is all about. But how are you going to do this "growing up" if you are not free to do so? Let's address this freedom thing—unless we have independence within we are not going to have much freedom on the outside.

I am going to change the questions for myself, and for you. Let's not ask ourselves what it is you are doing after school or what it is I do now for a living. Let's gauge our day-to-day life by another point of focus. Let's ask ourselves if we are *free* today. *Are you free* to create that poem or idea, free to be with those you love, free to paint, free to speak up, free to enjoy your work, free to travel, free to learn, or even free to be still? *Are you free* to move away and start something new? *Are you free* to create a dream of life after school?

Within this freedom is born all of our dreams. Use of this freedom may upset the apple cart, may put others out, may mean having less of one thing but more of something else. This freedom will give you the space and energy to be what your spirit intended for you all along. Freedom allows us to choose our actions based on our truth, rather than letting circumstances choose for us. Without

"Safety is all well and good: I prefer freedom."

—FROM *THE TRUMPET OF THE SWAN* BY E. B. WHITE, CHILDREN'S AUTHOR

Inside You Is the World

133

this freedom we may be walking someone else's path. Without this freedom our dreams don't have legs. Without this freedom we are not open enough to know what is real for us—that each day is a new dawn of possibilities.

I leave you with this meditation to practice in your "free" time.

- *Sit quietly with your eyes closed. Let your breath be slow and relaxed.*
- *Imagine the lower part of your body as a warm, moist, vital soil.*
- *Visualize a lotus growing out of the center of this soil. Picture the lotus blooming in your heart center.*
- *Breathe into the center of the lotus and repeat several times: "I am willing to embody my freedom."*

❖

✳ Are you free today?
✳ Write about boredom.
✳ A lotus grows out of mud and muck. Write about this.
✳ Imagine visiting a friend in prison. Write about it.
✳ Write about being real.
✳ Write about a detour you took and where you ended up.

Off the Page

Go outside in a quiet place where you will be undisturbed for at least thirty minutes. Listen to the sounds of nature. Let yourself go. Relax in this place. Remember how nature always provides a path for every one of its creatures. Then, in your own way, pray. Pray for guidance. Pray for help. Relax into this space, and know that everything true in the universe wants to help you be free.

"Now I pray that each and every being's true nature be revealed, that we each see clearly our inherent truth and find liberation from the shackles of suffering and difficulty imposed by the limitations of our mind."

—CHAGDUD TULKU,
TIBETAN BUDDHIST
WRITER

Inside You Is the World

Lavish waves.
Sometimes it's been hard.
It feels like a glorious dream.
The best part . . .
I Know it's Real.

—TAYANNE KLINER, HYPNOTHERAPIST

AND MEDITATION TEACHER

I Have Seen the Future and It Is . . .

I realized early on that part of my essential nature includes seeing the possibilities held in our collective future. I learned some utopian principles in graduate school and how to use these to envision and create a hopeful future. If my utopian view of the world is a real possibility, I thought, why do so many movies and stories of the future tell of doom, darkness, death, and despair? Why do the machines take over, or the aliens destroy cities? Sometimes we humans prevail in these stories but only by rebuilding a new world from the one that was destroyed. How is it we see ourselves destroying what we have?

It makes sense to me now that we envision the future as a black hole that sucks in everything beautiful. We are in Utopia *now*. There is enough of everything to go around today. If we shared the way we were taught in kindergarten we would all be fine. But we don't share. We are not cooperatively waiting in line either. We are pushing the person in front of us. *There are bullies running the recess grounds!* We are being naughty students and getting away with it. We're in the Garden of Eden, and we don't appreciate it. We know that at some time we will have to go to detention hall for all our wrongdoings— but like children, we don't want to ruin our fun now. So we project this awareness of impending detention (doom and disaster) into our movies and stories about the future.

If our thoughts and words have power (and I know they do), *rethinking* the future may be a great and necessary act for each one of us. At the same time we need to take responsibility for the condition

"This world needs Utopias as it needs fairy stories. It does not matter so much where we are going, as long as we are making consciously for some definite goal. And a Utopia, however strange or fanciful, is the only possible beacon upon the uncharted seas of the distant future."

—HENDRIK WILLEM VAN LOON, PH.D.,
DUTCH-AMERICAN
AUTHOR, HISTORIAN

of the planet today. Act now, *today*—while dreaming and creating a green, lively, thriving future.

> "I don't wish to defend everything that has been done in the name of Utopia. As I have tried to suggest, Utopia is not mainly about providing detailed blueprints for social reconstruction. It is about making us think about possible worlds. It is about inventing and imagining worlds for our contemplation and delight. It opens up our minds to the possibilities of the human condition."
>
> —HANS MAGNUS ENZENBERGER, TWENTIETH-CENTURY GERMAN AUTHOR

> "Without the Utopians of other times, men would still live in caves, miserable and naked. It was Utopians who traced the lines of the first City. . . . Out of generous dreams come beneficial realities. Utopia is the principle of all progress, and the essay into a better future."
>
> —ANATOLE FRANCE, FRENCH NOVELIST AND JOURNALIST

✷ Write about Utopia.

✷ Practice being a utopian thinker. Write how the next ten years of your life are going to turn out—positively. Include all aspects of your life: relationships, career, creativity, social activity, political expression, sexuality, spirituality, and so on.

✷ Now help create a *global* future. Practice being a utopian futurist for the planet. How will life look fifty years from now? What are the *possibilities?* Imagine, create—and help us all step into this world of possibility. Thomas Paine said, "It takes only one person to change the world." This person can be you.

> "If you don't know the kind of person I am
> and I don't know the kind of person you are
> a pattern that others made may prevail in the world."
>
> —WILLIAM STAFFORD, POET

"Why did they call it World War I, unless they knew it was the first of a series."

—PAUL KRASSNER, AMERICAN HUMORIST AND SATIRIST

Inside You Is the World

136

8

The Big Design

The Way It Is

There's a thread you follow. It goes among
things that change. But it doesn't change.
People wonder about what you are pursuing.
You have to explain about the thread.
But it is hard for others to see.
While you hold it you can't get lost.
Tragedies happen; people get hurt
or die; and you suffer and get old.
Nothing you do can stop time's unfolding.
You don't ever let go of the thread.

—**WILLIAM STAFFORD**

"We are each spinning our individual threads, lending texture,
color, pattern, to the 'big design' that is serving us all."
—**KAREN CASEY, AMERICAN AUTHOR**

The Way It Is

"You may feel far from it [true self], but it is never far from you."

—LAMA SURYA DAS, POET, AUTHOR, BUDDHIST SPIRITUAL TEACHER

Journals provide a tapestry of your life. When you read through them, you discover so much about your path, your dreams, your stories. Each journal entry becomes a thread, connecting you to all the other journal entries, and to every event in your life. Find a thread in your journal and pull on it, and an entire story unfolds before you. Even when it may be a sad story, you feel somehow stronger by gaining this knowledge. This strength comes from the connection we experience to our real selves through our journals—we see how everything we write matters and is linked together to reveal patterns. Your journal entries can be a thread from your past to your future, a way to rediscover your most authentic feelings and insights. As you continue to write about your days and your experiences in your journals, you can see the threads of your truth weaving throughout your life.

Friday, Nov. 20, 1992

We had our football awards night last night. Those things for football take forever but it's worth it to us players. I'm happy to say that at the end of the season I had accomplished more than just my goal. My goal was to make all-conference so I could get my name on the wall and to get a unanimous vote for most valuable Offensive Tackle. But I also earned an award for being on the first quarter honor roll while participating in football. But the most surprising thing was when I tied with Jake Deaver for Most Valuable Player. I hadn't even thought of that. So I was quite happy with myself and I am going to miss Stillman Valley football very much. These four years just flew by!!!

—MICHAEL Z., AGE 17, SENIOR YEAR JOURNAL ENTRY

And from Michael ten years later . . .

I read through my senior year journal in awe. It was a time that I completely focused on training and making myself into a masterpiece. I led by example and by always striving to better myself and the team. At the end of the year I had been awarded Team Captain, All-Conference, and MVP in football and wrestling. I placed first in wrestling sectionals only after upsetting the number one, two, and three seeded wrestlers in state rankings. The state champ Danny Deavers had a record of 29-1. I was the one person he didn't defeat. I placed fourth at state championships in wrestling. I received the Principal's Leadership Award, and the Sons of the American Revolution award, and was voted male athlete of the year. I also made the honor roll throughout the year.

Part of myself knew that I would never have this opportunity again so I repressed a lot of feelings such as pride in my accomplishment, enjoyment of success, and recognition of hard work. I felt it was easy to be great in a small school but knew this was just one phase of my life and I mentally rushed myself into the next as quickly as possible so I wouldn't get stuck in identifying with my high school accomplishments. I felt like if I acknowledged them then I would be stuck in the past and not able to do comparable things later.

Instead of acknowledging the greatness of me and what I have the capability of doing when I truly focus, I deliberately separated myself from that. Reading over my journal and sharing my story with a circle of friends, I realize it is time to take pride in all that I was and am. It is important to slow down and enjoy who and what you are today, right now. I wish I hadn't "rushed" myself through high school and had allowed myself to enjoy all my accomplishments.

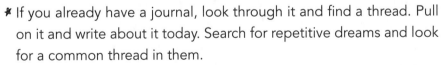

* If you already have a journal, look through it and find a thread. Pull on it and write about it today. Search for repetitive dreams and look for a common thread in them.
* What difficulty keeps arising? Have you solved it yet? How does this thread connect your past, present, and possible future? What does the thread tell you about yourself today? Michael decided to appreciate himself more in the moment. Write about the new insights that arise as you read your journal.
* Write about a thread that makes you feel good.

Just an Average Girl

Below is an account of a childhood experience as I wrote about it in my young adult journal when I was nineteen, followed by my reflection on it now.

8 a.m., August 1976

I walked this particular route home from grade school almost every warm day. It became a familiar and safe shortcut through one corner of deep woods. My feet would usually be covered with damp grass and dirt by the time I reached home. Out of the woods I would cross a yard that in the late spring would be covered with dandelions. As they are to most children, dandelions were beautiful to me, free flowers for the picking. Mixed in with the dandelions were Indian Paintbrushes. This day I grabbed a handful of both to offer my mother on my arrival home from fifth grade. In one hand I had the flowers, quickly folding over on themselves, and in the other my fifth grade report card.

It astonishes me how hopeful I felt as I picked the flowers and carried them home. I fantasized about my mother's reaction as she received these gifts.

But that day I also carried home my report card. Covered in C's I felt unsure of myself. C . . . C stands for "Can't." Can't do better. Can't expect more. The C's seemed to scream, like a silent shout, "she's average, just average."

When I got home my mother was in the laundry room. I put both my hands out and she took the report card and flowers. She opened up the report card and with no disappointment on her face said, "Some of us are C people, Julie, don't expect to do better than C's." Am I still that C kid, now, in my second semester of college? I feel so average. Yet not. How am I going to get by? At least she wasn't disappointed in me. Wasn't she good not to be disappointed in me?

Thirty Years Later

As an adult and a mother myself, I realize that in college I thought my mother correct in not being disappointed with me. And as a child and young adult I wasn't really upset at her considering me as "average,' just a C. Yet I remembered this incident enough to journal about it.

What does this thread tell me now? The truth is that when I pull on this thread now, throughout my thirty years of journaling I find some painful insights. I discover that even in my dreams my mother never thought of me as much more than a C person.

Following this thread I observed other strands of insight. There was my ability to trust and believe in myself even when those around me couldn't. I saw how I had learned not to go to the hardware store for fruit salad—meaning, don't go to someone for support and love when they don't have it to give. Go where you will get it. I found the thread of undying curiosity for truth. I found the thread that was my search for my own truth. All these are threads weaving in and out of my journal entries involving my mother. They are all threads to my true nature. They all tell me something of value about my life and myself. As painful as it may be at times to look back on my experiences, without them I would be missing an intimate and colorful part of my tapestry, my life.

---

* How are you extraordinary? What do others not know about you that makes you extraordinary? Write about this.
* Write about a memory you have about your mother.
* Do you remember bringing home a report card? What happened? What feelings and thoughts did you have when your parent(s) read your report card?
* Do you remember your walk or bus ride home on any particular day? Write about that.
* Just pull on a thread that you find in one entry, and reflect on it. Give yourself at least an hour to sit privately in your room with your journals searching for entries tied together by this thread. Yours may be connected to your mother, or your pets, or your teachers. Pull on one . . . and find out.

Invisible Threads

Synchronicity, defined by psychologist Carl Jung as "meaningful coincidence," brings into focus our invisible connections to the Big Design (what some call the Tao, that invisible unifying principle that

"When I don't write, I feel my world shrinking . . . I feel I lose my fire, my color."

—FROM *THE DIARY OF ANAÏS NIN* VOL. 2

connects us all) and to one another. I have shared in my other books many synchronistic events that were threaded throughout my life. Each synchronistic encounter anchored me to something within myself, and to something greater than myself. These events allowed me to experience the bigger picture—the web of life of which we are all a part. Even seemingly small encounters become a link to that which connects us all.

> "What is known intuitively, through experience of the Tao, is that we are not lonely, isolated, insignificant, and meaningless creatures, accidentally evolved from organic rubbish on a miniscule dot in the vast cosmos. Instead, the Tao experience gives us the direct knowledge that we are linked to all others and to the universe; through that which underlies everything and which some call God. Synchronistic events are glimpses into this underlying oneness, which is the meaning conveyed through an uncanny coincidence."
> —FROM *THE TAO OF PSYCHOLOGY* BY JEAN SHINODA BOLEN, M.D., JUNGIAN ANALYST AND AUTHOR

One aspect of a synchronistic encounter is that the outer "accident" is connected to some emotional or psychological situation you are experiencing internally. For example, I was concerned about my future, and praying about it, when a chance encounter intervened.

I was nineteen. I had applied for admission to the University of Wisconsin in Madison and I was not accepted. The woman at the admissions office said that my application was rejected because I didn't have enough algebra credits on my high-school transcript. I left the building very upset and confused. Up until that point I had believed that I was meant to go to college, that I was meant to become a social worker and maybe even write a book someday. Now what was I going to do?

I left the admissions office discouraged but not hopeless. I sent out a prayer to Spirit. "What now?" I asked. I walked over to a local drugstore that had one of the last remaining soda fountains and ordered a Coke. As I sat at the counter, worried but also trying to consider my options, someone took the seat next to me.

And who do you think it was?

It was my high-school algebra teacher! I told him about my situation, and he said that he would write a letter and set it straight with the university that I had taken enough algebra credits. Later that month I began my journey into higher education, ultimately going to graduate school and writing several books.

Recording these synchronistic encounters gives me a reference to all the times the invisible thread that connects us all has become visible in my life. At these times I feel my place in the Big Design. Whenever I wonder how to keep going, I remember my repetitive dreams and encounters or the times when rejection seemed to lead me to the place I needed to be.

Three times different friends mentioned this particular book to me. And then I was sitting in the coffee shop at Barnes and Noble and I was trying to remember the name of the book but couldn't. Two women sat down next to me and began talking about this amazing book (which, by the way, is not a big seller or that well known). I looked over and they both had the book my friends mentioned to me! I got up and had to order the book because the two women had taken the last two. I have since read the book, and yes, it was exactly what I needed at the time.
—CYN, AGE 18

* Start paying attention to meaningful coincidences—synchronicities—in your life, and record them in your journal.
* What is your internal world like right now? What meaningful coincidence can you imagine that could be connected with this?

I don't know where to go to college. It may sound like a small thing, but I am really confused. Should I stay near home (where my ex-boyfriend is), or should I move away? Both are scary. My meaningful coincidence would be to meet up with someone who really loved staying or going. . . . Or, I would meet

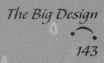

The Big Design

someone who graduated from the away college. Then I would know where to go. I would feel supported and less scared.

—NADINE, AGE 17, GRADUATING HIGH SCHOOL IN A FEW MONTHS

✻ "There are no accidents." Write about this.
✻ Write about the best unexpected encounter you have ever had with someone.

Our Threads Intertwine

"Sometimes our light goes out but is blown into flame by another human being. Each of us owes deepest thanks to those who have rekindled this light."

—ALBERT SCHWEITZER, GERMAN THEOLOGIAN,
PHYSICIAN, MUSICIAN, AND MORALIST

You, too, are someone's thread, his or her link to the Big Design. Through meeting up with you, they become aware of the divine connection that links us all. Just recently I received a letter from a woman who knew me during her teen years. I picked her up one late night, as she walked alone. I offered her a ride and a place to sleep. Here is how her letter (thirty years later) began:

"About a million years ago, I was a teenager—and you were a young woman of saintly patience and intense curiosity. We struck up a friendship which spanned my entire adolescence until I faded into a period of no mailing addresses. Recently, I wrote a young adult novel, which is soon to be published, and I thought: of all the people who have touched my life, Julie Johnson is the one who had the greatest impact, and I would like so much to share this book with her."

I later found out that her novel is based on her teen journals (!) and that she has kept a journal since the age of thirteen. See the thread?

In the cherry blossom's shade there's no such thing as a stranger.

—ISSA, JAPANESE HAIKU POET

It continues to weave through my life, as her letter helped me not to give up on this book about journaling. I had reached a low point in my writing. I felt discouraged and wondered, what is the point of writing yet another book that may or may not get into the hands of teens? I lost myself in the question that arises now and again for most of us—do my life and my efforts really matter? Then this woman's letter arrived. As I read the letter several times, I felt the heart and soul of this book, and knew that my life does matter. The message from her (and the Divine) that journaling through our teen years is worthwhile came to me loud and clear. She helped me see the thread that connects us all. I got a clear picture of the Big Design: that, for me, it only really matters that I reach one person—you. A thread exists between you and me as you read these words and hold this book in your hands.

* Your life matters. How do you know this to be true? Write about this.
* Write about someone who has had a positive impact on your life.
* Write a thank-you to someone.
* Write about what led you to this book.
* Write about a recent encounter (a nonromantic one).
* Find a spider's web somewhere and write about what you see.
* Write about a past encounter that is significant for you today.
* Many of your encounters today will be links to your future. How? Write about one possibility.

Inside of Us

Inside this clay jug are canyons and pine mountains
And the maker of canyons and pine mountains.
All seven oceans are inside, and hundreds of millions of
stars.

*The acid that tests gold is there, and the one who
judges jewels,
And the music from the strings no one touches,
and the source of all water.
If you want the truth, I will tell you the truth,
Friend, listen: the God whom I love is inside.*

—"THE CLAY JUG" BY KABIR, 15TH-CENTURY
HINDU MYSTIC, SUFI POET

I enjoy reading this poem over again a few times each time I read it. It reminds me of how we are connected to everything. It reminds me how deep and endless this unity is; it offers me a sense of my place and purpose. It reminds me that each life, whatever form it takes, is allied to every other living thing. The very oceans are within us; the sun, the mountains, and the moon. We each carry within us all life. Each of us is like the clay jug.

✱ Pick something . . . the clothes you wear (who made them?), or the furniture you are sitting on, or the lamp you are reading by, or the journal you are writing in—and *write about what is inside of it.* It can be written as a poem, a list, or simply a flow of ideas.

Inside this piece of paper is the sun and tree and the seed that made the tree. Inside the seed is the idea of the tree and the paper company who cut the tree.

✱ What is inside of you?

*"I am myself and what is around me, and
if I do not save it, it shall not save me."*

—JOSÉ ORTEGA Y GASSET, SPANISH PHILOSOPHER, SOCIAL CRITIC

✱ What does the above quote mean to you?

Threads Across Time

There are many days I don't want to be fifteen. No adult really wants to hear this—they just assume we will get through it. Or worse, when we look all put together on the outside, they assume the inside is fine too. Some days my insides are a mess, other days are better. Mostly I want to be out of high school, out of this fifteen-year-old body, over my acne, and out and on my way, somewhere away from here.

—TERITIA, AGE 15

With our journals we can travel in time—back to our past and into our future. I can go back thirty years and read about my thoughts, feelings, intuitions, and experiences and reflect on how they led me to where I am now. I can read about how I perceived and experienced my friends, or falling in love, or how I thought others saw me.

You have a big, mysterious, and beautiful future that awaits you. Okay, okay, there will probably be times of difficulty and, for some, great challenges. Yet the future is bright—trust me on this. Not one of my difficulties or challenges stopped me from having a big, beautiful life, and yours won't stop you either.

Meeting my future self was one of the most powerful encounters recorded in my journal. If you are having doubts about your future self, take some time to do this meditation. Have someone read it out loud, or record it and listen to the tape. Give yourself ten to fifteen minutes for this meditation. You may be seated or lying down in a comfortable position for this journey.

◉

Close your eyes and notice your breathing. Just let the breath move by itself. . . . Begin to follow your breath in and out of your nostrils, noticing how it brushes against the top of your nostrils as it moves in and moves out. . . . With each exhalation let your body relax . . . relax and breathe. . . . Now imagine yourself in your favorite place in nature. Notice the soft white of a few clouds passing by in the blue sky. . . . Breathe and relax. . . .

"Look, then write it down. Look again, you are everywhere."

—FLAMING RAINBOW WOMAN, SPIRITUAL TEACHER

The Big Design

Now notice that way, way off in the distance an adult is approaching you. This adult that you cannot really see yet is you. The adult you is walking toward you, has come back to visit with you and to let you know that your future awaits you. . . . This adult you has reached his or her full potential. . . . Your adult self is full of wisdom, and trusts and acts on your intuition. Let this adult you come closer, and stand together in this place in nature that you so enjoy. . . . Notice how he or she looks . . . strong and beautiful, self-assured. Begin to talk with him or her, and ask whatever it is you would like to know about your future self. Notice and take in all that you are shown. . . . You may see scenes from your future life. Just notice and ask any questions you may have. Reach out and touch this future self, feel the texture and warmth of your adult skin. . . . Spend two to five minutes asking your questions, experiencing this future self.

Then say good-bye to your future self and let her or him return to the future. . . . Let your adult self go, knowing you can bring her or him back anytime to visit. Now begin again to notice yourself there alone in your favorite place in nature, feeling stronger and more confident about yourself and your future. . . . Return your awareness to your breath, noticing how it moves in and out. Feel your body on the chair or floor and silently count to ten. Gradually open your eyes and return slowly and fully to the present moment.

Write in your journal about your visit with your future self.

Being yourself is your greatest asset. Spiritual journaling helps you create your self, your destiny, because every time you write (no matter what it is) you bring yourself to the page. You listen to yourself. You focus on who you are and what you want. When you take the time to listen to yourself, you feel connected to what is within you and to what is without.

For five years of my life, my journal was my best friend. I usually hid it under my bed or carried it around in my backpack. When I was scared, which seemed like a lot of the time, I wrote about it. I really wonder if I would be here today if I didn't keep a journal.

I also collected all sorts of stuff in it—pictures, CD covers, leaves, notes, magazine articles. My journal was more than a friend, actually—it was a part of me, the part that I had to keep alive at all costs. It was like those model babies that they give you at school to practice parenting with. Only this was my soul, and feeding it kept me alive.

—REBEKAH, AGE 20

Your life experiences, your feelings and intuitions, your encounters and mistakes are all part of your soul's journey and are all part of the Big Design. Right now, this moment, is bound to all the other moments in your life. The more we journal, the more we get a view of our life's path, of our soul's intentions, and of who we are and where we belong.

❖

* Write about being fifteen (no matter what your age now).
* Write about the age you wish you were.
* Write a letter to your future self. It can be for your next birthday or some date in the next five years. It can be to yourself when you are away at college. Write about your wishes right now, and include a couple of questions you have about yourself and your life. Include those things that are getting your attention. What are you spending your time and energy on? Who are your friends, and why? Have you been disappointed lately? Try to fill at least two pages.
* Seal the envelope, and on the outside write the date when you want yourself to open it. You can simply keep it in your journal or tucked away in a drawer. Or (and this can be fun) give it to someone who you trust will send it to you on the date written on the envelope. It can be quite remarkable to get a letter from yourself.
* Write to a past self that was hurting and could have used your wisdom and love.

"We believe in the respect for the interdependent web of all existence of which we are a part."

—UNITARIAN PRINCIPLE #7

The Big Design

149

Small Acts Make a Big Difference

A man was jogging down the beach after a major storm had just come through the area. He was dismayed by the huge number of starfish that the storm had washed up on the beach. He thought that there was nothing he could do because of the immense numbers. As he continued down the beach he saw an old man throw something into the water. As he got closer, he saw the old man walk a little farther down the beach, bend over, pick up a starfish, and throw it back into the water. As the jogger approached, the old man stopped again, bent over, picked up another starfish, and was about to throw it into the water. The jogger stopped and asked, "Why are you doing that? There are thousands of starfish on the beach. You can't possibly make a difference." The old man looked at the starfish, threw it back into the water, and then replied, "I made a difference to that one, didn't I?"

—adapted from The Star Thrower *by Loren Eisely (1907–77), anthropologist, writer, journal keeper*

We don't have to make a *big* difference to make a *real* difference. Consider the following true story.

One day, a depressed young woman went for a walk. She left behind in her room a suicide note, written in her journal, that expressed how unloved she felt. Recently a close friend of hers had gone into the hospital because of a drug addiction, her mother and father were considering divorce, and she was doing very poorly in school. She was in a lot of pain and wanted the pain to stop.

She decided that she was going to throw herself off a bridge. She walked for about half a mile to a bridge traveled by many cars and pedestrians. It was the end of a busy workday for most people and she passed by many stressed-out and unhappy faces. This made her feel worse and even more hopeless.

As she approached the center of the bridge, a man with a briefcase was coming toward her. He, too, looked tired. She saw that he still had his tie on as their paths were about to cross. They caught each other's eyes and the man smiled a big, wide smile, right at her, and said, "Why, hello." She felt his smile and greeting pour like warm sunshine right into her heart.

When she returned home that night she wrote a note in her journal: "If God could find a way to send me an angel to smile at me, I can find a way not to give up."

Sometimes it just takes a smile; remembering and saying someone's name; writing a thank-you note; following through on a promise; calling a friend who is sick. Life is mostly made up of small, real differences. It is all the small ingredients that go into making our favorite dessert that make it such a treat. Without even one ingredient, it might not be edible, much less tasty. Small matters.

* Make a list of ways you can make a difference.
* Write about who has made a difference for you lately.

Off the Page

Take this idea into the world now. How can you make a small difference today? Go ahead and make this difference and then write about it tonight.

The Big Design

9

Getting in the Flow of Writing and Life

Purple

In the first grade Mrs. Lohr
Said my purple teepee
Wasn't realistic enough
That purple was no color
For a tent
That purple was a color
For people who died,
That my drawing wasn't good enough
To hang with the others.

I walked back to my seat
Counting the swish swish swishes
Of my baggy corduroy trousers.
With a black crayon nightfall came

To my purple tent
In the middle of the afternoon.

In the second grade Mr. Barta
Said draw anything
He didn't care what.

I left my paper blank
And when he came around
To my desk
My heart beat like a tom tom.
He touched my head
And in a soft voice said
The snowfall
How clean
And white
And beautiful.

—**Alexis Rotella**, artist, poet

Spellbound
The World,
while spinning free
at The Dark of The Moon,
falls under a spell when The Moon
is New.

—**Raven Hail**, **Cherokee** elder, from ***Ravensong***

Opening Lines

Opening lines in a book or a poem are what pull you in to read the entire piece. We also have opening lines for our day (our first chosen thought), for when we meet someone (what we say beyond hello), and in our letters. All these opening lines have significant influence on what is to follow. I have learned to really listen to a person's "hello" and what follows it to gain quick insight into his or her intentions. I looked at first dates as the "opening lines" to that new person and trusted what I heard and experienced on that first encounter.

Each section in this journaling book has an opening line, as does each paragraph. It is this line that gets you to stay and read more, or makes you move on to another part.

Here are the opening lines for two of my other books:

"I am going to share with you a secret. A family secret."

"The journey into adulthood is the intended time to claim the Warrior's way. All the intensity, beauty, difficulty, and questions of the Thundering Years (the teen years) are designed to challenge us to determine what path we are going to take in life."

Here are the opening lines from a letter I sent to a friend more than twenty years ago. (She kept all my letters and sent them back to me as a gift.) *Dear Shannon, I am writing you on a warm and wet October morning. Everything seems changed.*

In some African tribes the first sound that a child makes, its cry, is echoed back by all the other children so that the child knows that she has arrived; the child knows that he belongs. This practice reflects the tribe's belief that without this first call back to a newborn the child will feel lost his or her entire life, searching for a sense of belonging. This cry is the child's opening line.

✦

✱ What might be an opening line for your book? Write some opening lines down (whether or not you have a book idea). Consider both fiction and nonfiction ideas.

"He didn't like her until he saw her with Jacob Crow."

"Her parents crashed the illegal party just in time to see Desa put a large bandage on her leg."

"Last night was a mistake."

"I have found that anything is possible."

✳ Then, if you like, expand on an opening line. . . . What happens next? Maybe you have a whole scene here, or a first chapter to a book.

✳ Now take one of your opening lines and write a couple of pages from it.

✳ You've just met someone. How are you introduced?

✳ Here are the opening lines from the bestselling novel *The Lovely Bones*:* "My name is Salmon, like the fish; first name, Susie. I was fourteen when I was murdered on December 6th, 1973." Write the next two lines. What happens?

✳ What is an opening line for you—for this day, today? Write that.

Off the Page

Jean Reddemann suggests that we start each day with this first thought: "Thank-you, Creator, for this new day. Please take me to where you want me to be." You too may want to start your day with prayer-like first lines. What would yours be?

Choose some favorite books and copy their opening lines. Write something different—what would you have happen?

In The Flow—Don't Think!

"Too many of us get stuck because we think we should know where to start and which ideas to develop. When we find we don't, we become anxious and either force things or quit. We forget to wonder, leaving ourselves open to what might come. Wondering means it's

"I'm exaggerating so you'll get to know me faster."

—AMY HEMPEL, AMERICAN FICTION WRITER

---

* *The Lovely Bones* by Alice Sebold, published by Back Bay Books, New York, 2002.

acceptable not to know, and it is the natural state at the beginning of all creative acts, as recent brain research shows."

—FROM *WRITING THE NATURAL WAY* BY GABRIELE LUSSER RICO,

CREATIVE WRITING CONSULTANT

Often the best way to write in a journal (as well as in first drafts of books and while brainstorming ideas) is to write quickly, without stopping to think. A sure way to get unstuck from fear or doubt is to *move*. If you are stuck and don't know what to do or what to write about, get up and put on some music, move around, breathe . . . go for a walk, jump up and down.

While journaling, if you find yourself drawing a blank simply rewrite a previous sentence until an idea comes. This helps keep the thinking mind out of the way, and keeps the pen moving on the page. It's a simple and miraculous way to get the creative juices flowing. For example, you want to write about being sorry. You might write repeatedly, "I am sorry about . . ." You keep repeating this phrase instead of stopping your pen or gazing off to think. This can actually be a very effective way to write about something. Get the beginning of one line that encapsulates the overall idea and repeat that until you have filled up at least one page.

✻ Pretend we are just meeting each other for the first time. Write something about yourself. Here is the phrase to repeat: "What you should know about me is . . ." (You can shorten it to "You should know . . .")
✻ What is something that brings you a great deal of happiness? Write about that. Use this repetitive phrase: "I am happiest when . . ."
✻ Write about something you would rather not talk to anyone about. Use this repetitive sentence starter: "I don't want to talk about . . ."

I don't want to talk about my friend who didn't show up at the party this past Friday. I don't want to talk about how she and I are going in different directions. I don't want to talk about how my breasts are too big

Getting in the Flow of Writing and Life

for the rest of my body and how I can't play basketball because of them. I don't want to talk about my friends who drink every weekend and I don't want to talk about how I am not really excited about turning seventeen in two months. I don't want to talk about the colleges I am supposed to be considering and I don't want to talk about how I don't know what I am going to do this summer.

—DESA, AGE 16

* Write about your mornings. Repeat the words "Every morning . . ."
* Write about a time you were stuck somewhere and wanted to get out.

Confronting the Empty Page

What to write? That's often the question that confronts me when I approach an empty page. But like so many aspects of the writing life, the empty page can show up in other areas of your life besides writing.

Your "empty page" may be a journal page, an unwritten idea, an empty canvas, or it may be this very day that stretches before you. This blankness, this emptiness, can hold such intense power that often we will move ourselves in a direction that takes us away from this emptiness—this Unknown—and into the Known. Personally, I find myself wanting to eat something when the blank page stares back at me. (Those Oreo cookies are calling me right now.) In certain times of our life when we are confronted with a lot of unknowns, a lot of blank pages, we give in to addictive behaviors with food, drugs and alcohol, tobacco, relationships, television, video games. A behavior is *addictive* when you can't control yourself and the craving or behavior just takes over. You lose your sense of choice and just give in to the behavior.

When the prospect of the blank page or the empty day, summer vacation or the end of high school, or the dark night looms in front of you, what are your usual responses? What pulls you away from

"The whole difference between construction and creation is exactly this: that a thing constructed can only be loved after it is constructed; but a thing created is loved before it exists."

—CHARLES DICKENS,
VICTORIAN-ERA NOVELIST

this Great Unknown and the present moment into a routine, or an addiction? What are your favored habits that seduce you away from the creative energy of the empty page or open sky? How do you deal with a big empty page or a day with no plans? Or, after a breakup, how do you deal with more alone time? Do you rush to fill it up?

When you take the time to notice what pulls you away, this awareness can aid in your return to the emptiness, and to the creative response to that emptiness. *It will return you to the possibilities inherent in the moment.* There is a lot trying to pull you away from the creative tension of the moment. Once we begin a dance with the emptiness by *remaining with it,* the present moment becomes filled with possibilities, and habitual patterns are at least quieted to a background buzz. (The Oreos can wait.)

* Write about this moment.
* What pulls you away from the Great Unknown, the empty page?
* How have you dealt with the unknown in the past?
* What is unknown to you, right now?
* What are you looking for?
* Write about addictions.
* Write about falling off the cliff and building your wings on the way down.
* Make a list of all the possibilities that scare you.

Mind Mapping: Getting Unstuck

> "Perhaps the greatest advantage of mind mapping is that by nurturing your unique, individual self-expression it guides you to discover your own originality."
>
> —FROM *HOW TO THINK LIKE LEONARDO DA VINCI*
> BY MICHAEL J. GELB

Mind mapping, or clustering, is a technique used by many writers to help them draw from the creative side of the brain to generate

new ideas. It is also used by people in all walks of life (including students!) to tap into a wider range of options for problem solving. Whenever you're stuck, or just want to stretch your mind further than it will reach at the moment, try this approach. Have you noticed that when you are frustrated or angry it is sometimes difficult to see anything but the bad? Mind mapping opens your mind and gets you out of being stuck and obsessed about what is going wrong, so that you can see what you might do to help things go right.

The technique is a form of word association that frees up the more creative, intuitive part of the brain (the right hemisphere). It reveals a wider view of the world. Here is what you will need:

- A blank sheet of paper (preferably one without lines). You could use an art pad (the bigger the paper, the better).
- Several colored pens, markers, or pencils. I prefer markers because they flow easiest.
- About ten minutes of time without distractions.

Begin by choosing a word. Put the word or idea in the center of the page and draw a circle around it. Then draw a line out from the circle and write the first word that comes to your mind when you think about your one central word. Circle this word. Then allow another thought or word to arise from that word, draw a line from the last word to the new one and circle it. Continue doing this until you feel you've come to the end of that particular stream of words. Now return to the original word you began your mind map with and begin another series of associations. Breathe throughout this exercise. Don't stop to think; write as quickly as possible. Don't stop moving your writing hand. Always write down the first word that comes into your head.

Remember to let the words just stream out of you, not stopping to filter your thoughts or judge them. This activates the creative part of your brain and awakens your intuitive nature. A lot of what you know sits just below your conscious mind, and clustering allows you to get to it. After mind mapping for a while, you will experience

"In most lives insight has been accidental. We wait for it as a primitive man awaited lightning for a fire."

—FROM *THE AQUARIAN CONSPIRACY* BY MARILYN FERGUSON, PUBLISHER OF *BRAIN/MIND BULLETIN*

Getting in the Flow of Writing and Life

an intuitive shift and possibly a desire to write about what your map displays.

Jerika, age 17, clustered around *Next Time*. She was feeling unhappy about how she had handled a recent situation involving a friend. She said, "Clustering helped me to be more honest with myself. I need to change how I do a few things in my life."

Here's a word to start with: *Graduation*. Circle it, and then begin to map!

* Take a look at your map of words—what does it say to you? Write about that.
* Map around:
    fear
    high-school hallways
    a hungry tiger

worries

hopes and dreams

next time

✱ Mind map around something you are stuck on. It could be a decision about a relationship, or what to do next in your life.

Off the Page

Read *Writing the Natural Way* by Gabriele Lusser Rico to learn her unique approach to mind mapping, as well as other techniques for releasing your "inner writer."

The Power of Lists

Make a list of every dream, every idea, every goal, every wish and desire you have had so far in your life. Don't stop writing until you have come up with at least a hundred different ideas, curiosities, or dreams. Most of them will be somewhat small, and some will be big—like traveling to India and living in an ashram for a year. You have the rest of your life to accomplish these. And chances are you will add quite a bit to your list as you go along.

Here's the beginning of seventeen-year-old Jessie's list:

talk to new people at school

go to Canada this summer (a road trip with friends)

get some new pants

try a yoga class

call Stephanie

break up with Adam

call my dad

surprise my sister

get a job

travel to a lot of foreign countries

"I write out of curiosity and bewilderment."

—WILLIAM TREVOR, IRISH NOVELIST AND SHORT STORY WRITER

Getting in the Flow of Writing and Life

learn how to live simply

eat more vegetables

eat less sugar

return K's phone calls

Lists are great. Lists are a way to allow yourself to get into a creative and natural flow. Write lists in the morning and then go about your day. Lists free you up to create more—sometimes from that list, sometimes something new.

✦

✶ Give yourself five minutes for each of the following:

List any regrets you have.

List all the friends you ever had.

List your favorite smells.

Write the wish list of a ten-year-old.

✶ Pretend you are now seventy-eight years old. Write what you wish you had done, but didn't do. (Just pretend you have regrets—you may not by then!)

✶ List your creative writing goals or intentions for the next five years. Prioritize them.

Accidents in Writing—and Life

Ever find yourself driving down the wrong road and ending up in a better place than you planned? Scientists in their research and spiritual students in their search look for accidents—in fact, they understand that some so-called accidents have a purpose. You have probably heard the term "Freudian Slip," meaning you say one thing when you meant to say something else. But the *accidental* comment perhaps revealed more truth than what you intended to say. A successful day has at least one accident that leads you down a path you might not otherwise have known was there.

This book, like my day-to-day life and my journals, is full of accidents that led me to something good, and often to something better. I find that accidents always point to something, and I let my atten-

"Life does not happen to us, it happens from us."

—Mike Wickett,
American scientist

Getting in the
Flow of Writing
and Life

162

tion follow what they are pointing to. Many famous novelists wait for the accidents in their writing, knowing that they will create the ultimate surprise scene. And in our day-to-day life, accidents can point to someone or some new idea that we may otherwise have overlooked. So when accidents happen, don't curse, don't whine, but *look*. Look for the golden key that may lead you to something of value.

The Golden Key

—by the Brothers Grimm, retold by Julie Tallard Johnson

There was once a young man who never seemed to have any luck. His parents were too poor to care for him, so he was sent off to live with strangers. Many times the strangers treated him badly. He had no time for friends because he had to work all the time just to keep himself fed.

One shivering winter's day he went searching for some wood for the fire. He had no gloves and practically nothing on his feet to keep away the bitter cold. He had traveled far from the house and it was so cold that his hands began to turn blue. He began to fear for his life and decided he could either give up and lie down to die or try to build himself a fire right there in the woods.

As he scraped away at the ice and snow, clearing a space for the fire, he found something—a golden key. Although he knew he might soon die from the cold without a fire, he thought, "Where there's a key, there's a lock!" and so he dug and dug with his bare hands through the frozen ground, until he found something again—a box.

"If only the key fits," he said, "my luck is sure to change!"

He looked for the lock, but he couldn't find it. It was dark and difficult to see. He nearly gave up when a voice deep inside him said, "Look again!" And so he did, and there it was, a keyhole so tiny you could scarcely see it. Most people would surely have missed it.

He took a breath and put the key in the lock, and it fit perfectly. He began to turn the key, and he opened the box and looked inside. He was so warmed by what he saw that the snow and ice melted around him. And indeed, his life from then on did change for the better.

"I may not know the key to success, but the key to failure is trying to please everybody."

—BILL COSBY, AFRICAN-AMERICAN COMEDIAN

Getting in the Flow of Writing and Life

163

❊ Write about what the young man found in the box.

> The box opened up into a hallway that led down into the ground. And the boy went in and hasn't been heard from since. But this is a good thing because he is in the Land of Creation, where possibilities are endless. It is also the place where the Frienders live.
>
> —Natalie, age 15, now writing a short story called "The Land of Creation"

> It is just an empty box. But maybe tomorrow it will be full of something magical.
>
> —Denise, age 17

❊ Write about a Freudian slip.
❊ Write about a recent accident.
❊ *It's not my fault.*
❊ Write about a premonition.

Off the Page

Look for accidents that lead to something better. Notice how accidents are part of the creative life.

Everything Worthwhile Is Borrowed

> "Genius borrows nobly."
> —**RALPH WALDO EMERSON, AMERICAN PHILOSOPHER, POET**

> "I do borrow from other writers shamelessly! I can only say in
> my defense, like the woman brought before the judge on a
> charge of kleptomania, 'I do steal, Your Honor, but only
> from the very best stores.'"
> —**THORNTON WILDER, AMERICAN NOVELIST AND DRAMATIST**

I know many teenagers and young adults who are stressed because they feel nothing new can be created. "Everything has already been done," one fifteen-year-old mentioned to me. "Yes, this is true," I told him, "but a great medicine woman from the Creek tribe once reminded me, 'Everything worthwhile is borrowed.'" In school they are often concerned about plagiarism. Borrowing an idea and adding your thoughts, your spin, to it in your journal is not plagiarism. Plagiarism is copying word for word or paraphrasing something someone else wrote *with no new input from you.*

I bring this up because these two concerns—worrying about plagiarism and that nothing feels new—can put you between a rock and a hard place.

Everything in this book is borrowed. The originality comes from what I do with it and what experience I glean from it. So, borrow away. Once you borrow some idea or story, make it your own. You add your bit of twist to it. You change the color, or add something, or take something away—and there you have something wonderful. You have something original.

❈

* Write about doing it differently. (Whatever "it" may be to you.)
* Write about the view from your classroom window.
* Write about being between a rock and a hard place.
* Borrow a good idea and put yourself into it. Purposefully borrow someone else's idea and make it your own. Then write about it.

> "I am a writer. I don't cook and I don't clean."
> —**DOROTHY WEST, AFRICAN-AMERICAN WRITER**

Getting in the Flow of Writing and Life

165

Throw Yourself In

> "Throw yourself into the hurly-burly of life. It doesn't matter how many mistakes you make, what unhappiness you have to undergo. It is all your material. . . . Don't wait for experience to come to you; go out after experience. Experience is your material."
>
> —W. Somerset Maugham, English writer, dramatist

As a writer you can draw materal from anything. That is one thing I love about being a writer: every conversation, the dream last night, the broken chair in the alley, the large man getting on the bus, the pencil on the floor—all are material for me to use in my writing.

In Buddhism there is a practice that suggests we be grateful to everything that shows up on our path. This is because everything and everyone can be used to wake us up to our true nature. This writing practice and this Buddhist principle can go hand in hand. Even the difficult stuff can have a place in your writing. You can write just to write, noticing whatever shows up on your path, or you can write *because* something difficult has shown up. I use the painful and silly stuff to get in touch with my true nature.

✦

✱ Using the following triggers, write just a couple of thoughts on each and then move on to the next one. After you have finished this first round of writing, go back and write more on any of these scenarios that you have more ideas about.

Farmers don't name their animals anymore.

Porches without swings . . .

The girl who wears pink every day . . .

You had been told all this before.

You hear two teachers talking and your name comes up.

He told you he was bisexual.

An unopened present in the middle of the garage . . .

> "Every fire is the same size when it starts."
>
> —Seneca proverb

Attending/not attending senior prom . . .
A friend is whispering to the new girl down the hall.
A missed opportunity . . .
She's/he's standing next to your locker.

The Art of Making a Fire

In indigenous cultures the art of making a fire was taught to the very young. Instead of hearing "hide the matches" or "don't touch that," children were given the skills to make fire on their own. In these cultures a child was given sticks, a knife, and dried grass and then his or her very own hands and breath created an ember that ignited a fire. This simple but powerful process linked the young with their own innate abilities to interact creatively with their environment. It did involve some danger. I am sure some got burned.

There are too many skills that we have lost over the ages—skills that used to help keep our creativity and self-esteem activated. These skills include building our own homes, candle making, learning many ways to use a knife, making bread and soup from scratch, writing letters, and archery, to name just a few.

But we still know how to use a few age-old skills. Rub the sticks together—bring pen to paper and light the empty page, and your life, with the fire of your words.

❖

✸ Write someone a letter (not an e-mail).
✸ Write about an old lost skill.
✸ Write about what you know.
✸ Imagine you live in the time when the young were taught to build fires. What happened when it was your turn to learn?
✸ Write about what was lost but is now found.

"We don't find what we are looking for at the mall."

—FROM *SEN 24/7* BY PHILIP TOSHIO SUDO, AWARD-WINNING JOURNALIST

From the Starbucks Bulletin Board

I do a lot of my journaling at coffee shops. Right now I am at the Starbucks in Madison, Wisconsin, with my writer's group. In this Starbucks, as at most coffee shops, hangs a bulletin board overflowing with announcements, business cards, notes, and flyers. You can discover a lot about your community, and yourself, from what is posted on the bulletin board. You can also get a lot of ideas for your journals, poetry, or novel from public bulletin boards.

To get a completely random subject for writing, I had my writing friend Dawn pick something off the board for me. It was an advertisement.

HELP!

Dead Battery • Keys locked in • Flat tire
Towing • Road Service

We still make house calls.

BOB GOAT ROAD SERVICE

HOME OF THE WORLD-FAMOUS CREW

608-222-2222
Locally owned and operated

Service Day and Night
7 days a week, every week

* Write about what makes them "world famous."
* Write about a time you were stranded and needed road service.
* After picking a flyer on a bulletin board, write about it.

Off the Page

Go around with some friends to coffee shops and other public gathering places that have bulletin boards and collect ideas for your poetry and creative writing. Take your journals with you.

Create a poster about yourself.

Eavesdropping

Eavesdropping can be a good thing. You can learn a lot from listening to people talk at a local coffee shop or restaurant. Eavesdrop and find out. I sometimes come up with a scene or idea for my fiction when listening in on a conversation. I once learned the history of the Mega Mall; another time I heard a group of young women pore over biblical quotes. You can learn something about other people's beliefs and, from your responses, learn something about yourself. The intention for this eavesdropping experience is an important one—to open up to new ideas to write about and to become more receptive to other's views. Please—no eavesdropping on friends or to be judgmental about what you hear. Simply listen in on a conversation as a writer— as a way into another's world. Listen, and write.

I am most interested in what boys have to say to one another. The conversations between women are not enough of a curiosity for me. Or maybe it is that I get enough of it in my life with friends. But what do boys visit about? Now this makes me curious enough to be still for a while and listen.

—NATALIE, AGE 16

"In writing, for the person who follows with trust and forgiveness what occurs to him, the world remains always ready and deep, an inexhaustible environment, with the combined vividness of an actuality and flexibility of a dream."

—FROM *WRITING THE AUSTRALIAN CRAWL* BY WILLIAM STAFFORD

I eavesdropped for a couple hours on a conversation I can say changed my life! It was a group of young men talking about their sexual identities. I was shocked at their openness. They had just left a PRIDE meeting and were very talkative. They might have guessed I was listening only they were totally engrossed with each other. I had so many questions about my own sexuality. I filled up six pages in my journal that night on what I heard and what I felt. This is only the start. What I am thinking and feeling will not go any further than my journal or my therapist's office until I know more about who I am and what I want.

—Brennan, age 15

* Eavesdrop on a conversation of strangers in a coffee shop or cafe. Bring your notepad and write as you listen.
* What would someone hear while eavesdropping on your latest conversation?
* Eavesdrop and use what you hear to write a short scene that could go into a story.

I didn't get all of their conversation but she was clearly less excited about getting together than the guy. She looked at her coffee cup and the table more than at him and wouldn't answer him directly when he invited her to go out that evening. She was stalling the inevitable. I would guess this was their second or third date and she wanted to end it before it went any further. I found myself feeling sorry for him. And wondered, Why is it so hard for us to just tell someone we aren't interested? I realized, sitting and listening and watching, that I am very scared about getting into a relationship that I will not want to continue. I am not very good at ending relationships either. She finally did get her message across but I didn't hear the specifics. He left first and she sat and drank a second cup of coffee, checking the place out. An idea for a short story or article came to me—one where the girl breaks up with the guy in a real obvious, and considerate, way. We could use more examples.

—Cassandra, age 23

10

In the Name of Love

Open Your Heart

Open your Heart!
Open your Heart!

Receive the love
That by your birth you're due

Feel the joy of love
Inside of You

Be the lily
Drinking up the moon

Be the rose
Fragrant in full bloom.

—JAMES POWELL, MUSICIAN, YOGI

"If love is the
answer, could you
please rephrase the
question?"

—WRITTEN BY JANE
WAGNER FOR LILY
TOMLIN'S ACT

Do you not see
That you and I
Are as the branches of one tree?
With your rejoicing
Comes my laughter;
With your sadness
Start my tears
Love,
Could life be otherwise
With you and me?

—TSU YEH, TSIN DYNASTY, 265–316 C.E.

Stolen Words

"In the beginning was the Word. And the Word was
with God and the Word was God."

—GOSPEL OF JOHN

Hippie, Christian, pagan, patriotic, gay, ritual, beautiful, Buddhist, family, love. These are just a few words I consider "stolen" words. A word becomes stolen when one group claims it as theirs, or we come to agree to one meaning of a word that actually takes it away from its true essence. *Love,* for example. I have heard this word routinely misused. Does love really mean never having to say you're sorry? Does it mean I always agree with you? Can it really mean, "This hurts me more than it hurts you?" What does it mean to love someone?

The longing that comes from loneliness is often mistaken for love. A young woman sat in my office this week and told me she got back with her boyfriend. He routinely puts her down; he controls her decisions; he deals drugs and threatens to harm her if she tries to leave him again. She says, "But I really love him. And he loves me." She found that it was very painful to be alone. Do you too believe that what she feels for him is love? Does he really love her? Is the word *love* being stolen?

- ✸ What words do you consider stolen? Write about one of them and through this writing begin to claim it back for yourself.
- ✸ How has *family* become a stolen word? What does the word *family* conjure up for you?
- ✸ *Love* is probably one of the most misused words. What does *love* mean for you?
- ✸ "Love is all there is." Write about that.
- ✸ You attend a gathering of friends and it turns out to be a ritual.
- ✸ Your best friend tells you she or he is Buddhist.
- ✸ Write about homophobia.

Mirror, Mirror . . .

Relationship is where most of our life takes place. It is where we hurt; where we grow; where we love; where we learn about ourselves. We all have many kinds of relationships. Some are intense and meaningful, others have less impact on us. Some are short-lived, while others span our lifetime. Relationships are essential to our personal and spiritual growth. Relationships are the true classroom of the soul, where we encounter all our hopes and fears. We find meaning and purpose in our lives through our relationships. Learning what love really is (not what the movies tell us it is) is a basic spiritual lesson, and one we all must learn. We learn about love in our relationships. And every relationship is a mirror of how we love ourselves.

Everyone in your life is your mirror. What this means is that *who* you are in relationship with says more about you than anything else. It is said that you are what you eat; in a similar way, you are what you see in your friends. So what do you see? Are they respectful? Then most likely you respect yourself. Are they kind? Mean? Do they gossip? Of course you tend to hang out with those who like to do what you like to do. Do they veg out in front of TV in their spare time or spend time being active outside? How well your friends take care of themselves tells you a lot about how well you take care of yourself.

We don't choose the family we are born into, but it too is our mirror. We learn first from our parents and siblings how to love, how to relate, and how to treat one another. And how we relate back to each of these people is a mirror for them.

* Who did you connect with today? Write about this. Describe the connection in as much detail as possible. Pick out one detail (a personality trait or a physical trait) about the other person and write as much about that as possible.
* Write about feeling disconnected.
* "You are what you eat."
* Write about your parents' relationship.
* Write about a time a friend went too far.
* My mother once told me . . .
* How are you different from your friends?

Fire Within: Letter to a Young Man

—by Mark Taylor, psychotherapist, writer, mentor of young men

Awakening to sexual awareness is a time when as a young man you come in contact with one of the most powerful sources of male energy. As with all forms of male energy, this sexualized energy has the power to create both good and bad effects. If misdirected, your sexual energy can be a source of danger not only to others, but to yourself. Directed in a good way, it can be a beacon.

Unfortunately, most young men are left to find their way through this mystical and potentially dangerous passage from boy to man on their own. Instead of having wise mentors and loving lessons, most American boys are left to figure out sex based on what they hear from older (and misinformed) peers.

It hasn't always been this way.

Ancient indigenous tribes around the world have known about the need to honor, celebrate, and channel this sexual energy in a

Fire has a love for
itself—
It wants to keep
burning.

—HAFIZ, SUFI MASTER
AND POET

In the Name
of Love

174

good direction. That's what lies at the heart of traditional rite of passage ceremonies. Tribal peoples knew that, left undirected, male sexual energy can—like an unattended fire—quickly flare out of control. Thoughtfully directed, it can lead the young man into intimate and satisfying relationships.

To the young men who found their way to these words: Don't waste yourselves on foolish or abusive displays of sexuality. This is a powerful fire you've been given. Whether this flame will be a beacon or a firestorm is up to you.

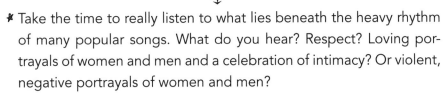

* Take the time to really listen to what lies beneath the heavy rhythm of many popular songs. What do you hear? Respect? Loving portrayals of women and men and a celebration of intimacy? Or violent, negative portrayals of women and men?
* Imagine yourself as an older person, and have this older, wiser self write a letter to your youthful self about your sexuality.
* Write about your first sexual experience (imagined or real).
* Write about what you know but were never told.

Off the Page

Find an adult male with both the wisdom and the compassion to provide you with guidance on channeling this potent energy in a good way. This could be a teacher, a coach, a family friend, or a therapist. Perhaps an uncle or a neighbor. You can also contact Mark on his Web site: Round-river2000.com.

Fire Within: Letter to a Young Woman

It's so simple but so important: Please don't give your self away. When you have sex with someone, you are not only exchanging potent bodily fluids, you are also exchanging powerful spiritual energy.

Consider this energy as fuel—if you give too much of it away, there will be nothing left for yourself. Each time you are with someone sexually, you give something of yourself to them. When there is mutual love and respect, a more balanced exchange is experienced. Even in a committed relationship, sexual energy is a very vital, valuable energy for you to share with this person, and it needs to be respected.

A young woman of fifteen recently spoke to me about her emerging sexual energy: "I thought I would wait till I got married or at least till I was out of high school and in a serious relationship before I had sex. And I wasn't all that interested in it anyway. But now it seems everyone is doing it. It makes me wonder what the big deal is. It makes me curious." What is the big deal? Are these girls giving it away or sharing something they realize is a precious part of themselves?

You *are* a sexual being. You have this energy to use in whatever way that you want. It is, of course, your choice whom to share yourself with and whom to withhold from. It is natural to be curious and to explore your sexuality. I hope for you all positive and healthy experiences. Be safe. Be conscious. And don't give yourself away.

* Write about sexual energy.
* Write about masturbation.

> Masturbate. Couldn't we come up with a better word? It sounds so nasty! Something you should not ever mention out loud. This is like another stolen word—but I can't seem to find one to replace it. Everything that comes to mind seems really silly or just as nasty. Maybe it is not the word that was stolen but the whole idea of it.
>
> —JESSICA, AGE 16

* The pregnancy test came back positive. . . .
* Write about your first sexual experience (imagined or real).
* Write about what you know but were never told.

An Old-Fashioned Wedding

With tattoos covering her strong body, a woman who was abused as a child and shared her precious beautiful body with too many men decides it is time to get married again. She considers, "What is the most important relationship for me? Who loves me? Whom do I love?"

Recently, at the age of twenty-five, she bought a chunk of land out in the country. She plans to build on it someday but for now she needs to live in the city, work, and save up more money. She sleeps out on her property on days off, getting to know every inch of this precious land. It also has tattoos, made both by man and by the Earth itself. All of it is beautiful.

She loves her land and the Mother Earth it is a part of. She feels love returned to her when she spends time outside, bare feet on the ground. Right now this love for the land is the most important relationship in her life.

So she decides to hold a wedding and commit her life to the great Mother Earth. Part of her ceremony is to offer up her dowry. She has created a box and filled it up with all her gifts and special talents, each one written on separate pieces of paper. These include her ability to drum, garden, and sing. Her box is full. I had known this woman for about a year and knew of only some of her many, many gifts. She sits in the middle of a circle of friends (all of whom love and respect her) and reads her list—offering it up to the Mother. It takes a good fifteen minutes for her to read all of her talents out loud. As she reads them, she feels love for herself rise up inside. With this love for herself, she knows she has a lot to offer the world. She then puts on a small silver ring to remind her of the commitment she is making to herself and to the Earth. This ring also reminds her of her dowry—the many gifts she brings into the world every day.

Now *this* is a love story. And it is one that will last her lifetime.

* Create your dowry—what are the gifts you offer the world?
* Who loves you?
* What is the most important relationship for you right now?

"For love is our true purpose, our true calling. Love is calling each of us home, to the vast reservoir of love within ourselves."

—LAMA SURYA DAS,
BUDDHIST AUTHOR
AND TEACHER

The Truth about Love

Is it possible to experience "true love"? Yes, but it may not look exactly like you might expect it to. Many psychologists and healers refer to it as "conscious love." Now that you are making your own choices about relationships, a healthy and realistic model of true love can help you make decisions that are right for you.

The most important ingredient in true love is individual growth. Yes! If you love someone, and someone loves you, you will encourage each other's individual growth. This holds true throughout your life. You will support each other's dreams and goals and allow room to change and grow. Whether the person you love is a friend, parent, or lover, inevitably you have to let that person go to do things that are important to him or her. True love, conscious love, supports your loved one's individual growth and personal empowerment.

For couples, true love encompasses more than just an infatuation with or attraction to the other. It includes all of these qualities:

- personal freedom for both people
- good communication on all levels—verbal, energetic, emotional
- individual space
- responsible behavior toward yourself and the other
- personal empowerment
- affinity and friendship
- compatible goals (but not necessarily the same goals)
- caring
- bliss (at times)
- delight in each other
- an ability to say no, and to say yes
- allowing the other to be negative as well as positive
- no coercion by either person
- nonpossesive behavior
- mutual understanding of the basis of attraction
- based in truth, not fantasy

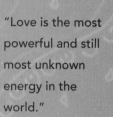

"Love is the most powerful and still most unknown energy in the world."

—Pierre Teilhard de Chardin, French paleontologist, Jesuit priest, writer

respect for both people's needs

knowing when it is time to move on and say good-bye

True love is more than just wanting that person to be "the one."

* Describe your ideal boyfriend or girlfriend. Try to include physical, emotional, and spiritual aspects. How will this person treat you? What goals will this person have for him- or herself?
* Write about the difference between fantasy and imagination when it comes to love.

> "I find myself fantasizing a lot about a certain person and never really following through on it and then find myself disappointed when nothing comes of it. Julie suggested I imagine what a great relationship would look like and then be open to finding that person. Rather than fantasizing about someone I met and getting it all wrong because my fantasy is so far from reality!"
>
> —KARYN, AGE 24

* Write about the best time you ever had with someone.
* Write a Dear John/Dear Jane letter in your journal. (If you're not familiar with this expression, it means a letter you send to break up with someone when you can't or don't want to do it in person.)
* Write about being possessed.
* Write about true love.

The Marrying Maiden

In the ancient Chinese oracle the I Ching, the fifty-fourth hexagram is often referred to as the Marrying Maiden. This particular hexagram would come up for me a lot in readings during my teens and twenties. It is about what happens if we rush into relationships, and it cautions us not to do this. Relationships have the tendency to bring out our deepest and strongest desires—for love, for attention, for recognition. Our desire to be the favorite, the first picked, the

"Sometimes a firm 'no' or 'I can't do that; it is beyond my limit' is the most spiritual thing we can say."

—FROM *A PATH WITH HEART* BY JACK KORNFIELD, BUDDHIST PSYCHOLOGIST, MEDITATION TEACHER

most important. Have you noticed how this is true? This is just the nature of relationships and being human.

However, if we act like the Marrying Maiden and rush blindly into relationships and let our desires push us, we often end up hurt or disappointed.

Anytime we rush into something, whether it's a relationship or an apparent resolution to a problem, we are likely to cause an accident. It is hard to really notice what is going on when we are rushing ourselves. And even though the Marrying Maiden has a feminie title, young men are also prone to rush into relationships, whether they be romantic, social, or work- or school related.

As I've mentioned before, at the age of sixteen I began to consult the I Ching and journal both my questions and its responses. When I followed its guidance, it always steered me in a positive, safe direction. But it was hard for me not to rush into relationships and commitments. Sometimes I just wanted to be with someone. I wanted the relationship to work out so I would "push" it to work out. But pushing relationships is like driving a car too fast. It is a lot harder to see what is really going on if you are moving too fast. And many car accidents result from speed and distractions.

Don't rush into a relationship, or rush it ahead too fast. Stay focused on what is going on and notice how you feel when you are with this person. Decrease your risk for accidents.

* Write about feeling rushed.
* Write about a time when you had a concern prior to doing something but did it anyway.
* Write about promises that were not kept.
* Write about a car accident.
* Write about being "sideswiped."
* Write about being a passenger in a speeding car.

"Why Do Girls Go for the Bad Boys?"

Someone asked me this question the other day—so I journaled my response.

I went for the naughty boys. In the seventh grade Bill came into my life. He is the first boy I kissed (and later married). He was and still is one of the nice guys. Back in the seventh grade he was my boyfriend for three months, until the bad boy from out of state moved to our town and attended our school. All the girls tried to get his attention. Even me. This did not sit well with Bill and he ended our relationship, abruptly. And the "bad boy" of the day chose my girlfriend Andrea.

We choose the bad boys because we think that love is something you have to earn and pursue. (Nice boys don't make you "pursue" them.)

We choose the bad boys to heal an original wound. In the jargon of psychology an original wound is a recurring feeling that stems from a painful experience in childhood (like feeling abandoned now because you were at one time abandoned as a child). We need to heal the problem from within first. But most of us go for getting the guy—*Maybe this time I will get his attention, love, approval. . . .* But it doesn't work this way. We must go to the source of the pain within ourselves and heal it, a process that requires the hard work of inner reflection, not focusing on getting affection from someone else. When we are able to do that, we no longer have a need for the "bad" boy.

We are attracted to the bad boy because he reminds us of all the characters in movies who were "bad" in a romantic sort of way. But that is only how it is in the movies. In real life we crash and burn and we don't always "get the guy."

Girls go for the bad boys because they haven't claimed who they truly are! If they don't see themselves as beautiful, smart, creative, powerful, strong, and

> "The nature of relationship is that it leads us into the desire state: we begin to desire another, desire recognition, desire retribution, desire a particular outcome."
>
> —BRIAN BROWNE WALKER, TRANSLATOR OF THE I CHING, WRITER

In the Name of Love

so on, they can be easily seduced and caught. A bad boy will be seductive and compliment the girl, making her feel special. Seduction is tricky. It speaks the truth (the girl is beautiful, smart, etc.), but it speaks the truth with a twist. The twist is that the boy wants something from the girl. He compliments her to get something from her (sex, control, prestige). Girls who know their strengths, their beauty, their gifts, are not seduced by compliments. When you know your own goodness, the compliments may feel nice—but they won't hold any power over you.

Naomi is a young woman engaged to a really nice guy and finishing up her undergraduate degree in journalism. She wrote down her thoughts on the subject.

I promised myself that I would NEVER do what I saw so many of my girlfriends do—break up with the really decent "nice" guy to obsess and chase after some guy who was not good and not interested in them anyway. But then I found myself totally into guys who were nice to everyone BUT me!

Now, at the age of twenty-three, I am finally with this really incredible guy. He is incredible because he treats me right! He is one of the nice guys. But I find myself thinking it won't last. Part of me figures he is just too nice—which translates into BORING! But, somehow I gave this guy a chance. Part of it was being hurt and burnt so many times by other guys I was just simply burnt OUT! All those times, putting my energy into trying to make someone like me—the wrong someone.

I found myself now, with this nice guy, relaxing a bit and then we started to have fun. I didn't have to always be pursuing him or trying to get him to like me. Or doing things with him that didn't feel right just to be with him. I realized how much of my energy and emotions used to go into this pursuit. Now we actually have time to be happy. I have energy for things like school, where before I was flunking out.

So, I figured out why girls don't go for the nice guys (they are out there!). I think that some of us only *feel* loved if we get our attention from some jerk because nice guys like everyone, are nice to everyone. This translates into "If he likes everyone what makes me special?" We don't want to be treated badly, we just want to be certain we are loved, that we are special. It is easier to feel this certainty when the guy is usually mean and then treats us well. Love in these relationships is then something we have to earn (which is why we are so tired all the time!). So bad guys prove we are lovable by being mean most of the time and then, now and again, "loving" us. This change in the bad guy (which by the way never lasts) "proves" that they love us and then we feel lovable.

Girls, give the nice guys a chance. Their love is real, it lasts and you have a LOT of energy left over for important things—like school, work, friends, or having fun together.

✳

* Write about nice guys.
* Write about seduction.
* Write about being special.
* Write about where you went wrong.
* Whose approval are you longing for?
* Write about being bored with someone.
* This older guy is hanging around the high school. . . .
* So, why are there bad boys?
* You were warned.

Animal Love: My Horses, My Teachers

—by Karen Braun, Horse Medicine Woman, animal healer, writer

On a not so nice day in November . . . cloudy, windy, chilly, I went outside to be with my four dear friends, my mares. They were milling around, searching for any last little nibble of hay that might be left on the almost frozen ground. Their lips are amazing . . . so large yet very nimble and able to separate out the tiniest morsel from the weeds and dirt. As I often do when I am feeling contemplative, I crouched down amongst my beauties and simply sat still with them. I watched. I listened.

One by one, they each came over to investigate me and say hello. Once comfortable with the fact that I had no carrots in my pockets, they each *walked away and continued to graze. Willow, the wise red mare, however, stayed longer. She proceeded to stand in such a way that she was behind me and her front legs were touching my back. Her neck and head reached out over my head so that when I looked up, there was this gorgeous neck of red fur looming over me, and the cute white spot on the bottom of her chin very visible to me. She sighed and rested a hind leg in total relaxation. As I sat there in this position that I would normally consider unsafe, I realized that Willow was guarding me as if I were her beloved foal. I looked up to see her eyes closed as she stood over me, protecting me like a mother. My heart melted with love and trust of her. I sat with her in this stillness for a while and then it began to drizzle and the wind picked up. Suddenly, Willow gently but firmly nudged me with her large head so that I almost fell over. She said to me, "You better go in now. You'll get cold." I stood up and kissed her on her soft white nose and went inside.*

* Write about your pet.
* Write about a horse's nose.
* Horses are wiser than people.
* The dog saved her life. . . .

Off the Page

You can find out more about Karen and her horse school, the Anam Cara School for Equine Bodywork, by e-mailing Kpbraun@chorus.net.

Forgiveness

1. to give up resentment against or the desire to punish; stop being angry with; pardon. 2. to give up all claim to punish or exact penalty for (an offense), overlook. 3. to conceal or remit (a debt).

Forgiveness Is:

- giving up any negative emotions that you are holding on to (and that are therefore harming you).
- freeing yourself of any hold or power that the offender may have over you in the form of your continued anger, resentment, or desire for revenge.*
- taking the time to express your feelings (to a trusted person or in your journal).
- a way to set clear boundaries between yourself and what someone did to you. *You are not defined by someone else's behavior.*
- being present for this moment and not stuck in the past.
- accepting yourself and others as fallible human beings.
- allowing an offense or trauma to be truly over.
- release.
- letting go.
- moving on.

Frankly some acts seem unforgivable—rape, incest, murder, abuse. But are they? What does it really mean to forgive? (Another stolen word.) How does not forgiving someone (or yourself) help with the pain of what happened?

The intent of forgiveness comes across clearly in *Webster's* definition above. It does not imply in any way that the behavior (the offense) is acceptable. Instead it focuses on giving up the resentment, the desire to punish, and the anger. This concept truly represents the beauty of and fundamental power behind forgiveness. *It essentially cancels your involvement with the offense.* Forgiveness is not about "changing your mind" about a particular experience or event, and it is not about "forgetting." It is not about accepting the other person back into your life or condoning his or her behavior. It

---

*Practicing seniority can be helpful with this (see pages 128–29.)

Blessed are the man and the woman who have grown beyond their greed and have put an end to their hatred and no longer nourish illusions. But they delight in the way things are and keep their hearts open, day and night. They are like trees planted near flowing rivers, which bear fruit when they are ready. Their leaves will not fall or wither. Everything they do will succeed.

—PSALM 1:3, HEBREW SCRIPTURES

In the Name of Love

is about gradually letting go of any fear, blame, anger, or any other intense emotion related to the offense. *It is about not carrying around all these negative feelings because of what someone else did.* (Or something you yourself did in the past.) Forgiveness is something that you are doing for yourself and not necessarily for anybody else.

What you will find when you refuse to forgive is that you are carrying the weight of all the negativity—the anger, the pain, the hurt, the memory—while the offender has forgotten all about it. Carrying it around won't affect the other person; it will only impact you.

- ✷ Write about the unforgivable.
- ✷ Write about your anger.
- ✷ Whom do you need to forgive?
- ✷ Write about jealousy.
- ✷ If you could do it over again . . .
- ✷ Write about where you went wrong.
- ✷ Write about a time you held your tears.
- ✷ I'd forgive him/her but . . .

Off the Page

Practice the following forgiveness meditations. Give yourself at least fifteen minutes to do each meditation and some time afterward to journal. Forgiving Others is best done in a small group (or with a meditation teacher or therapist) with someone reading the meditation out loud. (If the offense is rape or something as traumatic, please do this with the help of a therapist.) Forgiving Yourself can be done alone or with others.

A hand moves, and
the fire's whirling
takes different
shapes:
All things change
when we do.
The first word, "Ah,"
blossoms into all
others.
Each of them is true.
—FROM "SINGING IMAGE
OF FIRE" BY KUKAI

Forgiving Others

Sit in a chair with both feet on the floor (legs uncrossed). Sit comfortably without slouching. Close your eyes and take five nice deep breaths. With each exhale, be willing to let go of whatever it is you are holding on to . . . then begin to just breathe naturally.

Conjure up as vivid a picture as you can of the person you are forgiving. You may want to bring a certain incident to mind for which you are forgiving them. Imagine telling this person how you would have preferred they behave (how they should have behaved). Recall all your feelings and thoughts. Recall all that you wished the person had or had not done. Allow all the feeling to come to the surface as, in your mind, you tell this person what they did wrong and how they should have behaved.

Repeat this part of the experience until you reawaken the feelings you had in the past. Intense feelings with painful memories may arise, so allow your counselor or spiritual teacher to assist you. Stay with these feelings. When you have come to the conclusion of the emotional release, visualize yourself saying something like this to the person: "This is how I wish you had behaved, this is how I would have preferred to be treated, but you were unable or unwilling to do this. This does not change my wish that you had acted differently, but I now release you. I forgive you. What you did holds no more power over me. I fully and freely release you. I let go of the pain of what you did. What you did holds no more power over me. I forgive you. I am free of the harm you caused me. I let you go." (Or, "I let the incident go.") Say these phrases or something like them until you feel satisfied and believe what you are saying. (To reach that point may take more than one session of doing this meditation.)

Return yourself to the present. Feel your feet on the floor and the breath moving through your body. Take a couple of deep breaths. Count down slowly from six to one, and on one, open your eyes.

"Of all the knowledge, the wise and good seek most to know themselves."
—WILLIAM SHAKESPEARE, 16TH-CENTURY ENGLISH PLAYWRIGHT AND POET

In the Name of Love

Whenever the person or the hurtful incident comes to mind, release it and say to yourself any of the following statements: "I have forgiven you"; "This situation is in the past and no longer hurts me"; "I am free of the harm you caused me. Be gone."

◉

Forgiving Yourself

Make sure to have your journal nearby and give yourself fifteen minutes to do the meditation and another fifteen to journal. You will need to have these directions recorded so you can listen to them, or they can be read out loud to you by a meditation teacher, therapist, or someone else that you trust.

Start by sitting in a relaxed position in a chair, with your feet on the floor. Close your eyes and take five nice deep breaths. On the inhale imagine filling yourself up with positive feelings of love; and on the exhale release any tension or self-judgment. Continue to breathe throughout this exercise.

From a point suspended in the air before you, imagine a larger "you." This larger, older you is a guardian ready to speak to you. So you are the child self sitting in the chair now, and your guardian self is standing in front of you. The guardian is loving, supportive, forgiving, protective of the younger, smaller you. The guardian knows everything about you. The guardian gives advice but isn't ever critical. You trust your guardian completely. It is the part of you that understands how the child in you feels scared and hurt, and it has the wisdom and insight to help you. The guardian accepts you completely and unconditionally.

Now tell the guardian whatever has made you feel guilty or ashamed. Tell the guardian what you feel you have done wrong. Tell him or her everything. Don't leave anything out—what wants to be forgiven in you?

When you have finished telling the guardian about the incident and all the feelings and thoughts that go with it, ask the guardian for forgiveness. Then sit back and listen to what the guardian has to say. Let the guardian forgive you (because he or she will naturally forgive you).

Receive this forgiveness from the guardian openly and willingly. Imagine yourself the small child listening to a loving, trusting parent. The parent is you. Trust what you hear.

After the guardian is finished forgiving you, begin to return your attention to the present. Thank the guardian and let him or her go. Take three deep breaths and stretch. Count backward from six to one and on the count of one, open your eyes.

Record in your journal the advice of your guardian.

✻ Write about confession.

Off the Page

Go and make a "confession." Go to a large tree somewhere nearby. Sit by this tree and confess all your "sins." Give it all over to the tree (see pages 105–7 for more on tree wisdom). Trust that the tree is listening. Then sit for a few quiet moments and let the tree's natural strength and wisdom into you. Know that your confession is real, and that you are forgiven. If you brought your journal (and of course you did!), take some time to write about your feelings during this experience in your journal.

Live in the present,
Do all the things that need to be done.
Do all the good you can each day.
The future will unfold.
—Peace Pilgrim, American peace advocate

"The mystical journey drives us into ourselves, to a sacred flame at our center."
—Marianne Williamson, American author, lecturer

11

Running Down the Hallways

"Annie Bananie,
My best friend,
Said we'd be friends to the end.
Made me brush my teeth with mud,
Sign my name in cockroach blood."
—FROM *ANNIE BANANIE* BY LEAH KOMAIKO

"Putting others down becomes a path to identity, a path
we would not need to walk if we knew who we are."
—FROM *A HIDDEN WHOLENESS* BY PARKER PALMER,
QUAKER AUTHOR AND EDUCATOR

Stranger in a Strange Place

A teen client came to me the other day and put into one sentence what being in her last year of high school is like: "We don't want to be here but we're not ready to go." The ease of being a junior has passed, as has the comfort of childhood. She still likes being a "kid" but wants to be trusted to make her own choices. She knows she is leaving school and home soon, but still she has another year of high school to negotiate. Ideally, this big transition from childhood dependence to young adult freedom is done in a way that can be repeated in other transitions throughout your life. There will be many times you will have to let go of one stage of life to move into another.

Morning verse recited in 5th through 8th grades in Waldorf Schools

*I look into the world
In which the sun is shining,
In which the stars are sparkling,
Where stones and stillness lie,
Where living plants are growing,
Where animals live in feeling,
Where man within the soul
Gives dwelling to the spirit.*

*I look into the soul
That lives within my being.
God's spirit lives and weaves
In sunlight and in soul light,
In world space there without,
In soul depths here within.
To Thee, Creator Spirit,
I turn my heart to ask
That strength and blessing*

"Every stone is different. No other stone exactly like it . . . God loves variety. In odd days like these . . . people study how to be all alike instead of how to be as different as they really are."

—MONICA SHANNON, AMERICAN AUTHOR, RECIPIENT OF 1935 NEWBERRY MEDAL

Running Down the Hallways

For learning and for work
May ever grow within me.

—RUDOLF STEINER, FOUNDER OF THE
WALDORF SCHOOLS, GERMAN PHILOSOPHER

Going back and reading these verses makes me sad. I remember how much I loved going to school at the Waldorf school. I miss it sooooo much.

I felt at such peace there. Everyone was one big community/family.

Now at the public school there seems to be so much negative energy—not that there isn't good too, but . . . There also seems to be a lot of separateness between everyone—unless it's just me. People complain more about all they have to do—and I just am realizing how much I have fallen into that.

I used to be so excited to go to school, and it just isn't the same anymore. I don't have that same love and drive. I still want to do well in school. It's just that now everything is based on the next test score and what percentile it falls in. I have a hard time with this because I often try really hard and don't do as well as someone who hardly tries. This makes me feel discouraged about school sometimes.

—AMANDA, AGE 18

* If you could say a prayer in school, what would it be?
* Write about doing well in school.
* Write about wanting to leave but not being ready to go.
* Write about second chances.
* What will you miss/not miss once you graduate?
* "The purpose of life is a life of purpose." What does this mean?
* Write about who you were a year ago.

Off the Page

Read the book or watch the movie *Finding Forester* by James Ellison. Read *The Sisterhood of the Traveling Pants* by Ann Brashares.

"When we learn how to be truly present with our joy and our sorrow, with our longing and our desires, layer upon layer of ourselves and the world are revealed."

—ORIAH MOUNTAIN DREAMER, CANADIAN WRITER, AUTHOR OF *INVITATION*

Shouting at the Page

A lion in a zoo,
Shut up in a cage,
Lives a life
Of Smothered rage.

—LANGSTON HUGHES, AFRICAN-AMERICAN POET, PLAYWRIGHT, AND HUMORIST

I have shouted at the page many, many times. Sometimes I write best when I am upset. I sit down and I shout at the page—I let it all out. Most times, I feel some shift in perspective, some resolution, after getting my thoughts and feelings out and looking at them on paper. This helps me find a way to deal with the difficulty.

When I write about my anger, hurt, and frustration in my journal, I don't worry about offending anyone. You can write whatever you want in your journal, releasing your negative energy without injuring others. Anger and frustration are necessary emotions. They need to be felt and expressed. They are both part of your humanity. It is what you do with these emotions that matters. "Smothered rage" may become depression and fester inside until it bursts into an emotional or physical illness, or it may be kept quiet only through damaging addictions, such as overeating or abusing drugs.

Frustration is a particularly robust emotion. There are two things you should know about frustration: it is always there for a reason (so trust this feeling), and it usually means it is time for a change. This change can take place inside of you (your attitude, your feelings) or outside of you (in your relationships and behaviors). When

"Every passage has its price."

—FROM *WHERE THE WILD GEESE GO* BY MEREDITH ANN PIERCE

we continue to try and make something fit that doesn't, we usually become more frustrated. So if you find yourself feeling frustrated, answer the following questions in your journal— and be ready to make some changes.

* Who's "got it wrong"?
* Who is not listening to you?
* Write about frustration using the following words: *relentless; never again; tomorrow; green; empty hallways.*
* Who disrespects you?
* Write about a visit to the zoo.
* Shout at the page.

> ## Off the Page
>
> When you find yourself frustrated and in need of some advice and guidance, consult an oracle (see pages 59–61). A good book that is not an oracle but offers great guidance is *Conversations with God for Teens* by Neale Donald Walsch.

Minefields in the Hallways

—by Michele Belisle, high-school crisis counselor, writer, wisdomkeeper

High school isn't forever. Hang in there.

Is your high school like the one where I work? Drama! Drama! *Drama!* Not a day goes by without a tearful visit to my office from a distraught young woman. She sits in my office sobbing, "I can't stand this place anymore! I hate the drama. It isn't fair. I can't even trust my friends. They're spreading rumors that aren't even true and everyone believes them. I hate being in the halls, it's the worst. What am I going to do? I just hate this place!"

For many teens, especially young women, going to school each day can feel like a daily walk or run through a drama minefield. There are many "drama bombs" just waiting to be tripped, only to explode in someone's face. Do you recognize some of these drama bombs—rumors, name calling, excluding, labeling, judging, gossip, put-downs, breakups, pressures, expectations, injustices?

It is normal to feel overwhelmed with the daily job of figuring out where these drama bombs are going to be, how to avoid them if possible, and what to do when one or more "explode" and disrupt your day, your life. Just knowing the minefield exists is a constant pressure. Even if you don't find yourself personally tripping over the drama bombs, you are affected each time others like you face the explosions. It can take a huge amount of energy to make your way each day through your high-school minefield. You may not be able to deactivate all these drama bombs since you can't always control their makers, but you do have the POWER to render them less powerful in your life.

There are many kinds of powerful "protective gear" you can put on to help with your daily walk or run down the hallways of your high school. The main thing to remember is that, whichever ones you choose to use, always make sure they are safe and healthy for you and those around you. Here is a suggested list of protective gear. You can add more ideas to the list.

Positive self-talk
Creating art
Reading this book
Journaling
Meditating
Having healthy relationships
Keeping a sense of humor
Standing up for yourself
Being Senior (see pages 128–29)
Becoming an activist for positive change in school
Maintaining your inner independence (see pages 126–27)

The Buddha said;
"See yourself in others
Then whom can you hurt?
What harm can you do?"

Volunteering

Practicing good self-care for your body

Taking long walks

Listening to music

Talking to a supportive and trusted person

✳

✸ Think about your own high school. What is your daily walk down the hallways like?

✸ Write about a recent drama bomb.

✸ Write about a rumor about yourself and the impact of this.

✸ Write about rumors.

✸ Imagine what your "protective gear" looks, feels, smells, tastes, and sounds like. Visualize yourself clothed in your protective gear, side-stepping and deactivating those drama bombs or staying powerful despite them. Make a pledge to yourself that you will not allow the high-school drama to define you, destroy you, or rob you of your spirit. Write it out and look at it each morning before school. What is your pledge to yourself? Take time to write it.

Refusing the Scripts

—by Michele Belisle

It is not really enough to just survive all this high-school drama stuff. Maybe it is really important to try to understand it so that life can feel more peaceful. After listening to so many young people telling me that it is just a part of school life and will never change, I now half-jokingly suggest to the students I counsel that if what they say is true then we ought to host a weekly High School Drama Fest. Each Monday morning students could pick up their "scripts" and have at it! We might as well charge admission and help the school budgets! This usually brings a nod and a smile and the comment that yes, it is pretty sad and ridiculous that there has to be so much school drama.

Unfortunately, so many young people believe that nothing can be done about this: *That's just the way it is, so get used to it, deal with it, and hope that you can survive it.* Sadly, many young people do not survive so well. Some find ways to drop out of school. Some find other ways to survive—withdrawing, becoming angry and striking back at others, acting in self-destructive ways, even joining forces with the drama bomb–makers.

So what is this drama stuff all about anyway? Once again I rely on the experts . . . you young people who help me understand it. Through the sharing of your stories you teach me that you often feel vulnerable and unsure of yourself at this age and that this feeling is scary. It can be difficult to find a way to communicate this fact, so it becomes easier to mask these feelings with behaviors like gossiping, labeling, judging, excluding, spreading rumors, and bullying. Maybe you want so much to feel like you belong to a group that you may resort to behaviors that aren't truly in keeping with your inner spirit, your true self.

You are very aware of how the media influence you to believe that if you don't look the "right" way then you are not okay and won't find happiness or success. The media even decides what it takes to have a satisfying relationship and we all know what the media says: the right labels, lots of money, the right body type, and the list goes on. Speaking of relationships, you make it very clear that there is pressure to be in one even if it is not a healthy one. How sad that it becomes more important to be in an unhealthy relationship with another person than in a healthy relationship with your own self.

We don't live in a perfect world so you are probably right about the fact that the daily school dramas will not go away; but—*you* do not have to *go away from yourself.* You have shown me that you have incredible energy, goodness, power, and spirit. You can use these gifts to help you turn down these drama scripts even if it is only one script at a time. You can help others to do the same. There is a quote on my wall that reads: *I am only one, but still I am one. I cannot do everything, but still I can do something. I will not refuse to do the something I can do. (Author Unknown)*

"You have brains in your head. You have feet in your shoes. You can steer yourself any direction you choose."

—FROM *OH, THE PLACES YOU'LL GO* BY DR. SEUSS, AMERICAN CHILDREN'S AUTHOR

Running Down the Hallways

* Write about a day without drama.
* Write about spin doctors.
* Remember what is good about you. Write a list of your gifts.
* "If you can't beat them, join them." Write about this.
* Have you ever been involved with instigating school drama? Spend some time reflecting on what needs you were trying to meet through this behavior. Was this honoring your true self?
* What is the "something" that you are willing to commit to in your effort to not participate in orchestrating school drama? Write this commitment in your journal.

> ## Off the Page
>
> It is most important that you honor what you know to be your truth. If at some point your school becomes an unsafe place for you to be, physically or emotionally, PLEASE don't stay stuck. Talk to trusted people—your folks, a school counselor, a teacher, or other supportive people. If it becomes necessary, explore alternative methods to get your education. If you are now in crisis, make this commitment—that you will not let another day go by without talking to someone who can help you figure out what to do. Good luck to you and peace always.

Sometimes it is best to keep our truths to ourselves. A teacher or some other adult may be the hungry tiger in your life—hungry for your dignity. This is a sad reality. If you have a hungry tiger in your life, write your truth in your journal, and walk safely away from the hungry tiger. Do your best to avoid such people and not engage in their "cat and mouse" game. Don't be a hungry tiger's meal.

"What you can do is often a simple matter of what you will do."

—FROM *THE PHANTOM TOLLBOOTH* BY NORTON JUSTER

Running Down the Hallways

"One does not contradict a hungry tiger."

—FROM *MY FATHER'S DRAGON* BY RUTH STILES GANNETT,
CHILDREN'S AUTHOR

Sacred Timing

"[A flower unfolds] slowly and gently, bit by bit in the sunshine,
and should too never be punished or driven, but unfold in its own
perfect timing to reveal its true wonder and beauty."

—EILEEN CADDY, FOUNDER OF FINDHORN,
A SPIRITUALLY BASED COMMUNITY IN SCOTLAND

We've all heard the expression *Timing is everything.* Discover and honor your own timing. It is uniquely yours and you must listen for and follow its rhythm, beat, speed, and pace. (Journaling helps you do this.) So often the timetable for the things you do is forced upon you. Many projects and expectations involving you are based on other people's timing. If you work for someone else, you are obliged to adhere to your boss's timing. If you are in school, you are obliged to comply with your teachers' and professors' timing. If you live with your parents, you must adhere to their timetable. You will always be interacting with the timing of others. But ultimately there will be much that is yours to choose.

You can begin to claim more of your sacred timing before you leave high school. Sacred timing is in tune with nature's clock. Your timing is unique to you—it is your own pace and rhythm for life. It is not something that is forced—it feels natural to you. What things can you claim now to be on your terms, your timing? You have to get a paper in to the teacher by Tuesday. Can you write it late at night, as you prefer to do? Are you a crammer or do you take your time with things? How much time do you want to give to this particular project?

"'What time will dinner be tonight?' said Frances.
'Half past six,' said Mother.
'Then I will have plenty of time to run away after dinner,' said Frances."

—FROM *A BABY SISTER FOR FRANCES* BY RUSSELL HOBAN, AMERICAN CHILDREN'S AUTHOR

My history teacher wants me to take his honors class my senior year. This is a great compliment but mostly it is a huge stress! He can be a good teacher, one I have learned a lot from—but basically it is his way or the highway. He is always right. Well, I know this isn't so.

He sometimes humiliates students. And this is wrong. He approached me in the hallway and "invited" me into this special class. Right there on the spot I declined. I was very polite and said no. He frowned at me and shook his head. He said he was very disappointed in me. But I felt great! He had complimented me by inviting me into his class but I took care of myself by saying no. I am already stressed out by my last year in high school. I have a lot on my plate already. This choice respects my timing.

He approached me again in the hallway and scolded me for not coming into his class. Julie reassured me that having this ability to take care of myself and not allowing myself to be pressured into doing what others want, doing things in my own way and according to my own timing, will help keep me healthy my entire life.

—TERESE, AGE 17, GRADUATING WITH HONORS AND UNDECIDED ABOUT COLLEGE

There are bigger timing issues ahead, such as when to go to college, when to get married, when to travel. I know a lot of parents who get uptight if their child doesn't want to attend college right out of high school. Perhaps you have another idea of what you want to do right out of school.

I just want to take a year off to feel what it is like to be out of school. This really freaks out my dad. He thinks if I don't go to college right away, I won't ever go. He said he regrets never getting his degree. And I'm afraid if I force myself to go to college right away I will hate it and then really blow my chances. I wish I knew what to do.

—REED, AGE 18

✴ Whose timing is affecting your life right now?
✴ Your parents think you are lazy. Write about that.

- Write out a list of your intentions for the next year. Now write out your parents' plans for you for the next year. Compare them.
- Write about perfectionism.
- What do you want to do the year following high school or college?
- Make a list of all your commitments. If you could choose, which ones would you let go of?
- Write about feeling rushed.
- "Timing is everything." Write about this.

Off the Page

Take a road trip to the closest nature preserve. Take your travel notebook with you and write about what is being preserved. Why do you think these things need preserving? Write about what needs preserving in you.

Waiting for Life to Happen

I teach a yearlong class on intuitive development and creativity. After the class has gone on for several months I look around the group to all the faces. Some students have expressed their hopes of "doing great," getting things done, making things happen. Some feel stuck, sad, or uncreative. Others are on the fence or have a mix of good and bad going on. Usually someone wants love to come into their life, while another is falling in love. I look at them and say: "Close your eyes for a moment and breathe. Think about your life *right now*, the good, the bad, the beautiful, the difficulties. . . . Just bring your attention to all this stuff going on inside and outside of you. I realize some of you are in a lot of pain and confusion. Try not to push it away; open up to whatever your life is, right here, right now."

After a few moments of silence I say, "This is what a creative life feels like, looks like. A creative life is *whatever your life is right now*."

"Ten thousand flowers in spring, the moon in autumn, a cool breeze in summer, snow in winter.
If your mind isn't clouded by unnecessary things, this is the best season of your life."

—WU-MEN, ZEN MASTER

You have gotten this far in this book. *You are living the creative life.* Your creative life looks like this . . . sometimes empty, sometimes full. Sometimes moving, sometimes stuck. There is no *one way* for the creative life to look or feel. Once you are open to your creative genius, your true nature, it is harder to close the door on it than it is to continue to open to it. You have come this far—there really is no going back.

Okay, let's say you did "go back"—you stopped writing in your journal, you stopped believing in yourself, you fell back into unhealthy habits. Maybe, like me, you didn't write, watched too much nighttime television, and ate too much salty food. Here's what happens then: The "going back to old ways" feels less real, less right, less fulfilling. You have already tasted the divine—you are not about to settle for less for very long.

* Write about settling.
* What is happening in your life right now? Write about that. (Don't forget to keep journaling about your day-to-day life throughout your journal.)
* Write about what it means for you to "go backward." What would this look like in your life?
* Write about being creative in school.
* Write about someone who was doing really well but is now having a lot of difficulty.
* What takes you away from your creativity?
* Write about someone you admire.
* Write about your best friend.
* Write about your last pair of shoes. Who is wearing them now?

Close your eyes and take a few moments to check in with yourself. Reflect on the idea that however you feel—whatever is happening—is part of living a creative life, walking a spiritual path.

Graduating Kindergarten: Life Lessons 101

It was difficult to let go of my only child three years ago and send her into the hands of strangers. Like many children, she had spent the first five years of her life almost exclusively with her father and me. Day after day we taught her about life, sometimes its basics (walking and talking), and sometimes its more mystical elements (where did Cayce, her pet dog, go when she died?). Public education felt scary to me (I am one of those adults who does not have favorable childhood memories of school).

But, of course, we let her go.

I thought the best way to really get a feel for what goes on at school was to volunteer in the classroom. The kindergarten teacher was gracious enough to let me come in and "help" during the last hour of class every Monday. It wasn't all that easy for me, at first. I was on the lookout for problems. But during this time I witnessed the beauty and power of teaching and got a small taste of what goes into a day of teaching kindergarteners. What surprised me most was that not only was my daughter learning the academic basics, but I found us both leaving with many life lessons learned.

I witnessed the teacher model the following values in her classroom:

- Don't gossip or tattle on others. (Only "tell" on others if they are in danger of some kind.)
- Focus on your own project, rather than have all your attention go to what others are or are *not* doing.

"Learning to listen to ourselves is a way of learning to love ourselves."

—JOAN BORYSENKO, PH.D., MEDITATION TEACHER, AUTHOR

- Try to stand in line without poking or kicking the persons near you.
- Learn through playing together.
- We don't all have to agree (it is okay if your favorite color is red and your friend's is blue).
- Everyone gets a chance to be the leader for the day.
- It is not okay to speak badly of others.
- Wait your turn.
- Practice patience.
- Try not to mix paints all together.
- Everything you create is wonderful.
- You don't have to share your personal toys; it is up to you.
- Notice how your behaviors and choices affect others.

In addition to gaining fresh meaning from these lessons, I witnessed the joy of teaching our children to read and listen to stories, to participate in something that benefits everyone, and to learn how to figure stuff out for themselves.

I don't know a lot about the teacher's life outside of school, but I know she has a full one. I know it includes raising children of her own; building a log home; kayaking; enjoying folk music; and being an active participant in her community. I am not only relieved that my daughter had an opportunity to be taught by such a fine human being but also grateful. I feel I graduated from kindergarten again myself, with some worthwhile life lessons.

- ✱ Write about your kindergarten teacher.
- ✱ What would your Life Lessons 101 include?
- ✱ The personal life of a teacher: imagine it and write about it.

Beginning Again

> Every fall I am psyched for school. . . . I feel ready to do better, even my clothes and outlook are new. Then I show up for the first class and instead of getting a new teacher, last year's history teacher sits at the front. And I sink, fast and deep. He doesn't like me, he thinks I am lazy (he has told me so) and I look up to see him frowning at me again. What's the use? I think. What's the point to start again if you keep returning to the same old stuff?
>
> —NATALIE, AGE 17

It can be a challenge to begin again if others around you hold on to an old image of you. You've seen how writing can be a way of "inventing" yourself. It can also help you to *reinvent* yourself.

Try this creative visualization (give yourself about five minutes). Sit in a comfortable position. Image a sign you carry taped to your chest. This "sign" is a message you send out to others—it is the energy people feel coming off you when they are around you. What does the sign on you say? Is it angry, kind, protective, judgmental? Is the message one that you want others to be reading?

We all carry these signs. Sometimes we have different ones for school, for home, for work, and for travel. When you become conscious of the message you are sending out, you will gain more understanding of the response you seem to be getting from others. This can influence their response to you and affect how you feel. Your sign carries with it intentions and energy. Energy always speaks the truth, and it is the energy of a person that we tend to respond to.

For years the invisible (energetic) sign on me read "F#*@ You." I was an angry young woman, especially when it came to authority. I thought this message was what I needed in order to protect myself. But its usefulness wore out quickly and I found myself getting a lot of negative responses from people. So, I decided somewhere in my mid-twenties to rethink the message I wanted to carry out to the world. I was still angry. I was still defensive and protective. But the hostility was melting and I felt more open to others, even to those in authority.

"We don't know who we are until we see what we can do."

—MARTHA GRIMES,
MYSTERY WRITER

So I changed my sign. I changed "F#*@ You" to "Don't mess with me." It is one of many I still carry. I know this message is read loud and clear in the places I wear it. I feel protected and confident—without triggering people's negativity. And people are much less likely to mistreat me.

* Rethink and rewrite your sign. Make a list to choose from in your journal.
* Try changing your sign for ten days. Consciously, each day, take down the old sign and wear a new one. Write about your experiences.
* "Energy speaks louder than words." Write about that.
* Write about beginning again tomorrow. What will be new, different, better?
* Write about moving to a new town and school.
* Write about the ideal place to live and go to school (real or imagined).

It's Zugenruhe!

"The way to find your true self is by restlessness and freedom."

—Brenda Ueland, American writer, author of If You Want to Write

Audubon defines the word *zugenruhe* as the restlessness that precedes migration. It forces the animal to migrate, pushes it on to its next destined place. This zugenruhe is just what animals (and humans) need to get them to take the next step. It helps the birds to migrate and can help you to make necessary changes.

Listen to your impatience, your restlessness. What does it want? What is it restless *for*? Impatience and restlessness have a negative rap. But as Brenda Ueland tells us, restlessness—and the freedom to see where it leads—are keys to unlocking your true self. Feelings of restlessness and impatience remind you of your desires and goals and push you to move toward them. If you find yourself feeling restless, listen to this feeling. What needs to change; where do you need to go? It may be your instinctual nature nudging you to take flight, to migrate on to the next place in your life. There are times throughout your life when your restlessness will arise to move you forward. If you are not feeling this restlessness at these times, such as during your senior year in high school, then you are probably doing things to numb yourself out.

You can either listen and respond to your restlessness or desensitize yourself to it (in which case it will hover under the surface). If you turn off your restlessness through substance abuse or by dulling it in other ways, you are silencing the call of Spirit, which wants to assist you in hidden and mysterious ways. You are numbing out something intuitive and instinctual that will help you attain your life's goals. Shutting yourself off from these sensations can result in depression and anxiety. These are natural and rhythmic feelings inside of you that you need to listen to in order to flourish in your life. Stop being comfortable with hanging out in the same old way, in the same old place, if it is time to move on. Venture out to new vistas. It is time to migrate!

* Write about a bird that forgot to migrate.
* Write about taking flight.
* Write about restlessness.
* Write about feeling impatient.

Off the Page

Watch the wonderful movie *Winged Migration*. Can you feel your own zugenruhe rise up inside of you?

To feel your zugenruhe, do one or more of the following for ten days: Take yourself off television; if you use drugs, alcohol, or even too much caffeine or sugar, stop during this time; spend at least five minutes in nature every day (include one morning sunrise); spend some quiet time with yourself everyday; journal every day. Get ready for zugenruhe!

"You don't need endless time and perfect conditions. Do it now. Do it today. Do it for twenty minutes and watch your heart start beating. . . . "
—BARBARA SHER, CAREER COUNSELOR, AUTHOR

Running Down the Hallways

12

Fire in the Lotus: When Life Becomes Difficult

Dusk
At dusk iridescence,
houses, trees, grass, flowers
begin to glow
Giving up the stored light of day.
Darkening sky
opens to us, a glimpse
into the heart of matter,
as it lapses into night.

—SHANNON KING, POET, ARTIST

"Life was suddenly too sad. And yet it was beautiful.
The beauty was dimmed when the sadness welled up.
And the beauty would be there again when the sadness went.
So the beauty and the sadness belonged together somehow."
—FROM *DOMINIC* BY WILLIAM STEIG, CHILDREN'S AUTHOR

Rejection as a Blessing

For the past twenty-five years I have been in the process of writing books. If rejection were a deterrent for me, I would not be a published author. In fact rejection and creativity go hand in hand. Rejection, as it turns out, brings to me the people, events, and places that are most crucial to my success. It can do the same for you.

In 1989 I went in search of a publisher for my first book. Three years later, and after hundreds of rejections (I could wallpaper my house with rejection slips), I got a nibble from a good publishing house. I worked with an editor for three months revising the manuscript. The next step was for the editorial board to approve the project. They all gave it thumbs up. They sent it on to the president of the publishing house—and he rejected the manuscript. He even went so far as to reject the entire concept of the book. So, after five years spent writing the initial manuscript, three years of rejections, and three months of rewrites, I decided to send it out *just one more time*. I made it clear to Spirit, the Great Unknown, that this was my last attempt. If my book was meant to be published, this was the time for a YES. If it was not accepted, then it was time to give up. Within a month, I came into my office at work and found a pink message slip that let me know Doubleday had called. They accepted my manuscript, and my life as a published author began.

Every rejection I have ever had (from boys, friends, publishers, teachers, family, organizations) led me to something greater, something bigger, something better. When we understand our rejections as *pointers,* as road signs directing us another way, we find ourselves in a place we are truly meant to be.

Many of my clients often mistake times of abundance as a "sure sign" that God or the universe is somehow working with them; that the spirits are pleased. In contrast, they experience lean times, or times of rejection, as the universe somehow working against them. You may not appreciate your rejections (as I have come to), but you can take the view that what *appears* as a rejection is only a way for

"After the final no there comes a Yes and upon that Yes the future world depends."

—WALLACE STEVENS,
20TH-CENTURY
AMERICAN POET

Fire in the Lotus

you to get to that more ideal place; a way for you to connect with something greater. Rejections are a favor from the universe.

Offer your thanks to all those who have rejected you and to those in the future who will say no to you. If not for them, you might have lingered longer in a place that was not meant for you.

There is a *yes* that awaits you behind every rejection. Trust me on this one.

* Write about a recent rejection.
* How might this recent rejection lead to something (or someone) better?
* Write about giving up on something for something else.
* Write about deciding to give one last chance to some person or project. (Then give it one last chance.)
* Write about something (or someone) you want but cannot have.

I cannot have Michael. He is going out with a good friend of mine. And I am involved with someone else, too. But Michael and I seem so perfect for one another. He respects me and I just enjoy myself when I am around him. I dream about him. I guess it is okay that I can't have him but the not having seems to make me think of him more and more. This bothers me to write this down. What if someone reads it? It upsets me to read it even though it is in my own head. I guess it makes it more real. I can't have a picture cell phone, either. I think I want what I can't have instead of being happy with what I do have. I'd better burn this journal when I'm done with it!

—NAME WITHHELD, AGE 18

What I want and cannot have is too much to mention and too appalling to put down in writing.

—AJAX, AGE 17, FUTURE CARTOONIST

The Right Road Lost

*Midway on our life's journey, I found myself
In dark woods, the right road lost.*

—FROM DANTE'S *INFERNO*

Any time I have taken someone else's path as my own, the mistakes I make are much more difficult to deal with. However, when I align with what feels true and right for *myself,* the difficulties I encounter on my own path are much more manageable. This is because when problems arise from my own choices and ideas they are truly mine to handle. When I give myself up to someone else's choices, I end up dealing with *their* trouble.

Have you ever let someone else make a choice for you that didn't really feel right? Like letting a friend make up your mind about who to go out with? Why is it so important to this other person that you do what they want? Has anyone tried to recruit you into their religious institution or their political cause? Have they used scare tactics to try to convince you? You may benefit from the ideas and suggestions of others, but in the end it is your path, your life.

I didn't really like the guy too much. And until my friend set us up, he didn't have much interest in me either. But she thought it would be really cool because her boyfriend and he were best friends. I cannot believe I have spent two and a half years with this guy doing things I really didn't want to do.

Finally, my mom kept asking me why I seemed so down all the time. She was worried about me. I read through my journals from the time I started going out with Peter and read how unhappy I was. I connected the dots and decided even if it meant I would lose a friend, I was going to break up with Peter. It was easier than I thought, and I didn't lose my girlfriend. But I am going back to doing some things I liked before, like riding lessons. And honestly, the boredom and sadness I feel at times is much better than the depression and headaches I had before. If you find yourself sad a lot or confused, read through your

"There are some things you learn best in calm, and some in storm."

—WILLA CATHER, AMERICAN NOVELIST

Fire in the Lotus

211

journal—you might find the answer there. And don't let anyone else pick your friends for you.

—ASHLEY, AGE 20

The moment I was told I would burn in hell if I didn't join them, I dropped them. I admit to feeling a little scared—why did they push this hell thing so much? But very quickly this threat of being left alone (left behind), this threat that I wouldn't belong anywhere good, even in the afterlife, if I didn't follow them, was seen for what it was—scare tactics to recruit members. This just didn't feel right. So, I ignored them and found new friends.

—LUCIA, AGE 18, WHO JOINED A CHURCH THAT DOESN'T
USE FEAR TO KEEP HER COMING BACK

* Write about a time you did something because someone else wanted you to.
* Write about being left behind.
* Write about peer pressure.
* Write about ending up in a place you wish you hadn't.
* Write about being recruited.

Off the Page

Attend the religious service of a faith other than your own, just to educate yourself on what else is available.

9/11

—by Stefanie Peters, age 18

I don't remember exactly what time the first plane hit the World Trade Center, because I didn't hear about what happened until about 9 a.m. that day. I was only a freshman in high school, and first period was relatively isolated in the band hall. By the time I found out what was happening, everyone was freaking out. There had been cryptic messages over the intercom from the principal. Frantic phone calls from our teacher's husband. My fellow students tried to explain. Everyone had a different theory. Everyone had heard part of the truth, but not the entire story. I decided that they were probably mistaken. Nothing as bad as what they were imagining could have happened. Impossible.

Our teacher suddenly began to cry. Her husband was relating the news reports to her over the phone. We all watched as she found pictures on the Internet and turned her monitor around to show us. Smoke was coming out of the side of a tall building. She pointed to the middle of it and said that it was a plane.

The pictures kept coming. More smoke. A second plane. And then suddenly, no more towers. I didn't understand. Wasn't it an accident?

It seemed so far removed from me. I would hear people say that we should all be enraged about this attack upon our people. I sure wasn't enraged. I didn't know anyone who died, or who was hurt. I didn't know anyone in New York. Texas seemed a world away from the rest of the United States. I began to wonder if I was the type of citizen that I should be. Should I care more? Was something wrong with me? Sure, I realized what a horrible thing it was, and I was sad that it happened, and I thought that we should respond.

I came to the conclusion that I'm probably not alone. I think that a lot of Americans are confused about what happened on 9/11, confused about the image our country holds in other countries. Confused about the direction we are going. 9/11 was my introduction to following current events and politics. You could say that I began to pay attention because maybe Texas isn't all that far from everything and everyone else.

Stefanie Peters lives in Texas and is studying literature. She is currently working on her novella *Lady Gypsy*. More information on Stefanie and her writing can be found at www.stefaniepeters.com.

Here is the poem she wrote after the towers fell:

Planes fly out of nowhere as I walk into 1st hour class—
A plane?—We bombed Israel! Lebanon! Didn't we?
Now everyone whispers. Fearful thoughts bloom out loud.
World War III begins today. Images on the TV—
Smoke. Fire. Crying. Why are you crying? Why?
The screen divides us.
The country is falling apart. My heart might be breaking
open.
You all say so.
Hundreds are dead. Thousands are dead.
Bodies jumping. Watchers gasp. I am a watcher.
Are they ok?
The towers collapse. I watch them fall. What really happened?
Lifeless photographs
I feel no pain. There are no tears. Just emptiness.
The repeated images. Repeat. *Look. Don't look*
We cannot go back.
To where?
What is happening?
Where is my fear? My heart is breaking open
out loud.
I'm only watching.

✱ What is 9/11 to you?
✱ Write about fear.
✱ Write about feeling safe in an unsafe world.
✱ Write a poem using the following words: *last chance; jumping; hidden meanings; piano lessons; refrigerator magnet.* Begin by writing

one sentence for each word or phrase, and then bring the sentences together somehow to create a poem. It is always possible to build something from very little or from items that appear completely unrelated.

* In chapter one, "Word Warriors," I write about the truth and lies in written history. What should the history books say about 9/11?
* What tragedy feels far removed from you?
* What is your personal 9/11? When did change in your life seem that sudden and traumatic? This would be a time that you will never forget—that maybe, in some ways, even defines you.

My personal 9/11 was the day I got my MS diagnosis.

—DAVID, AGE 24

My personal 9/11 is when my parents separated. Even though I know it happens to fifty percent of marriages, they seemed to get along okay. I thought they loved each other. Everything changed the day my dad moved into his own apartment. I felt like I was truly clueless about what was going on around me. I felt hollow but had to pretend I wasn't surprised.

—CECILIA, AGE 15

My personal 9/11? I don't have one. Does everyone have to have one? I feel very fortunate that my life has been good, safe, no big tragedies. But I feel both a little bit guilty and a little bit scared.

—JOCELYN, AGE 17

Never Give Up

The blizzard of the world
has crossed the threshold
and it has overturned
the order of the soul.

—LEONARD COHEN, POET, SONGWRITER

"There's a lot of hope and a lot of faith and love mixed up in a miracle."

—MEINDERT DEJONG,
CHILDREN'S AUTHOR

Sometimes it is just plain hard to be alive. Sometimes we think all we can do is give up, be discouraged. Even though the soul can (and does) go into hiding, it can never ever be destroyed completely. That is why I say *never give up*, because that ember that is the spark to your entire being is there (although it may be buried beneath a lot of rubble).

Sometimes instead of giving up we just need to rest, take a break, not make any big decisions. Consider this excerpt from Joseph Le Conte's "A Journal of Ramblings through the High Sierras of California," which relates the adventures of a university professor and a group of students on a backcountry camping trip in 1870.

Heavy clouds have been gathering for some time past. Low mutterings of thunder have also been heard. But we had already been so accustomed to the same, without rain, in the Yosemite, that we thought nothing of it. We had already saddled, and some had mounted, when the storm burst upon us. 'Our provisions—sugar, tea, salt, flour—must be kept dry!' shouted Hawkins. We hastily dismounted, constructed a sort of shed of blankets and Indian-rubber cloths, and threw our provisions under it. Now commenced peal after peal of thunder in an almost continuous roar, and floods of rain. We all crept under the temporary shed, but not before we had gotten pretty well soaked. So much delayed that we were now debating—after the rain—whether we had not better remain here overnight. Some were urgent for pushing on, others equally so for staying.

Just at this juncture, when the debate ran high, a shout, "Hurrah!" turned all eyes in the same direction. Hawkins and Mr. Muir had scraped up the dry leaves underneath a huge prostrate tree, set fire and piled on fuel, and already, see!—a glorious blaze! This incident decided the question at once. With a shout, we ran for fuel, and piled on log after log, until the blaze rose twenty feet high. Before, shivering, crouching, and miserable; now joyous and gloriously happy.

* "These are the things happening that make me want to give up." Write about them.
* "I will not give up today because . . ." List at least ten things.

My thoughts and feelings are confusing . . . overwhelming. My spoken words, many times, just don't seem to come out right. I'm uncertain, unclear. Sometimes, when I journal, I start out just ranting, which is usually equally unclear. But most of the time, there's that ONE CLEAR THOUGHT that jumps from the page to tell me something about my situation or myself. That thought stands out so clear that when I look back on it, it hardly seems like the words came from within ME. I think when I write I access a deeper, clearer wisdom. I think if I took away all my emotional baggage, my fears and anxieties, the people who hurt me, the procrastination, the lies I tell myself, the things I haven't learned yet, the behaviors I need to change—if you stripped all that away, I think you'd see my core. *The person I'm looking for when I try to "find myself."* I know sometimes, that person whispers these words to me and I write them down.

—LIA JOY RUNDLE, AGE 21 AT THE TIME OF THIS JOURNAL ENTRY

* Write about the feelings and thoughts you are having right now.

> ## Off the Page
> Find a wilderness camp you can go to, or an expedition you can join.

"Follow your image as far as you can. Push yourself."

—NIKKI GIOVANNI,
AFRICAN-AMERICAN POET

Fire in the Lotus

The essential characteristic of a spiritual life (no matter what the religious focus) is that our problems become the very place to discover wisdom and love. From there, all the juicy stuff comes to us, creating a way for us to improve our lives and ourselves and to open our hearts even more. It is the fire in the lotus. The difficulties in our lives often make us who we are. It is the sand in the oyster shell that makes the pearl. Everyday trials hold this gift, this potential of waking up our hearts and making our lives better. Happiness is not about having or not having problems; it is about how we respond to them.

Both the spiritual life and the writer's life show you many ways to open up and learn from all your circumstances, rather than fight them, avoid them, or insist things progress a certain way. Typically, we think our problems are *outside* of ourselves . . . out there somewhere, caused by someone else—therefore, out of our reach to change and transform. But so often, difficulty really arises from our response to a given problem, not the problem itself.

Your difficulties require your most compassionate attention. Inner independence is born out of your ability to work with *any* energy or challenge that arises.

* Write about being cursed.
* How do you see and meet the daily difficulties that arise in your life—as a curse or as a blessing? Make a list of your difficulties and their causes.
* When you have difficulty with a friend or loved one, name that one thing that really bugs you about the other person. Write it down. Can you see this quality in yourself as well? Reflect on how you treat that part of yourself.

Finding the Dream in the Conflict

In every conflict there are dreams trying to come true. Pick a conflict that seems to repeat in your life. Do you know what it is you are wanting, dreaming about, in this situation? A conflict is two dreams of a perfect world colliding with each other. You may think that your bedroom would look fantastic in purple and black; your parents say lavender. And there is the conflict—you dream of purple and black walls; they dream of lavender. There is nothing inherently wrong here, just two different ideas of how something should look. You will find this to be the case with most conflicts: good people trying to have things go their way. It helps in such situations to spend some time considering: what might the other person's dream be?

> My mom and I fight about whether she can leave me alone at home. Her dream, I realize, is for me to be safe, to not rush into anything stupid. It is also for her not to be stressed all the time about what I am doing. The dream for me is to be trusted and to feel close to my mother while also feeling independent. Actually this exercise helps out a lot—I realize I am mostly focused on what I want, and why I want it. And I can only see that she is trying to stop me from getting what I want. I want her to trust me. And I see her dream in this conflict is to know and trust I will be safe.
>
> —KARA, AGE 15

* Take a few moments to journal a recent conflict. Describe as much about it as you can.
* What is your dream—what is it you were, or are, trying to fulfill in this scenario?
* What is the other person's dream?

"You gain strength, courage, and confidence by every experience in which you really stop to look fear in the face. . . . You must do the thing you think you cannot do."

—ELEANOR ROOSEVELT (1884–1962), FORMER FIRST LADY, ACTIVIST, AND HUMANITARIAN

The Lion and the Boar

—from Aesop's Fables

One hot summer day a lion and a boar arrived to drink at the same pool of water. They soon began to argue over who should drink first, and they ended up getting into a bloody fight. The fight became quite gruesome, with each animal receiving dreadful bites and scratches from the other.

All tired out, they stopped to catch their breath. While resting, the lion and the boar saw some vultures flying above. The vultures' mouths were watering as they wondered which of the two would end up a corpse on the ground.

At this point the two fighting looked at each other and decided to stop their bloody battle.

"It would be better to be friends and share some water," they said to each other, "than to become tasty morsels for vultures."

Even on Your Worst Days . . .

"You need to claim the events of your life to make yourself yours."
—ANNE WILSON-SCHAEF, PSYCHOTHERAPIST, LECTURER, WRITER

Even on your worst day you are surrounded by things you care about. Many times I have my clients who are depressed write a list in their journal each night of things they appreciate or care about. Sometimes the list is simple, sometimes it is complex. Jessica, who is eighteen, found that she was sad about fewer things than she was happy about: "My appreciation list got bigger when I started to really take the time to journal about those things I cared about each night. It didn't get rid of my sadness, but it definitely increased my happiness."

* Name four things presently in your life that you care about.
* Let's have some fun with this (play is always an antidote for a bad day). Describe each of the four things you wrote above in words you would not typically choose when describing them. For example, "I care about Allison who sits next to me in study hall" becomes "quiet time with green eyes, in a room of twenty still feet."

Now take the images and words you've conjured up and write a poem. Just let yourself play with it. Add some words if you want, move around the ones that you have, as I did below:

> Green eyes
> in rows of rooms and feet
> still
> some laughter
> and
> in the quiet
> I am saved.

Secrets

"I put a piece of paper under my pillow, and when I could not sleep I wrote in the dark."

—HENRY DAVID THOREAU, AMERICAN AUTHOR,
NATURALIST, TRANSCENDENTAL PHILOSOPHER

Writers are told all the time, "Write about your experiences, write about what you know." And what do we know better than the secrets we keep? It is no accident that every one of my published books, and most of the pages of my journals, hold my secrets. And it is by writing these secrets, these thoughts, these experiences, these ideas, that I am freed to live unburdened. I am set free because secrets get ugly and scary when you keep them in the dark.

"All growth is a leap in the dark, a spontaneous unpremeditated act without the benefit of experience."

—HENRY MILLER, 20TH-CENTURY AVANT-GARDE AMERICAN AUTHOR

Fire in the Lotus

You may not be ready to tell anyone your secrets, so your journal can hold on to them until you are ready. When you do write a secret down or tell someone something you have carried in your heart for a long time, it is let out into the world like a butterfly out of its cocoon. Free to migrate where it wishes. Your secrets will transform right on the page, from shadows wrapped in darkness to delicate, exquisite mosaics of color breaking free and flying into the light.

Often writing a secret that may be painful just to think about is a first step toward letting it take flight. After you have written it down in your journal, you may feel ready to let it go. (See forgiveness on pages 184–89).

❖

* Turn off the lights in your bedroom and make sure the room is pitch black. Now write at least one page in your journal in the dark. Look around you; what do you see in the dark?
* Write about secrets.
* If anyone knew this they would . . .
* In a place where there are other people present, take a look around you. Choose a friend or even a stranger sipping coffee; write about the secrets they keep.
* What do you think would surprise those closest to you if they knew it?
* Write about having an eating disorder.
* Write about a happy little secret.

The Secret Everyone Knows

My mother has cancer. She has had cancer since I was five, and I am now seventeen. The doctors told her that she would be dead five years ago. She is alive and strong these days. But everything around her is tainted by her cancer, her dying. Every time we get into a fight she reminds me that she has cancer. She reminds me of the song that she is going to have played at her funeral. She reminds me that she is going to die.

This cancer has owned my life. And in so many ways it is less real than anything—something that hangs out there like a lie someone told that won't go away. My mother runs my life, and her life, by the cancer.

She introduces herself to others with the opening line, "Hi, my name is so and so and I should be dead from cancer." The really odd thing is, and it is just awful of me to write this, but I truly believe my mother could not live without her cancer. My whole life I've only known my mother as a person who has cancer. I don't even know who my mother would be without it. I would live with my older brother if it weren't for the cancer—or maybe I want to live with him because of the cancer. All I know is in the center of my life is my mother's cancer. This is my dark little secret that isn't really a secret and it really isn't so little.

—TERESE, AGE 14

✷ Write about the secret everyone knows.

This is an easy one. My dad's alcoholism.—BRIAN, AGE 18

✷ A parent is diagnosed with cancer.
✷ Write about a miracle.

Off the Page

Go rock climbing (check local sport stores for rock walls). Write about the experience.

Can't You Just Leave Me Alone?

When life's at its darkest and everything's black,
I don't want my friends to come patting my back.
I scorn consolation, can't they let me alone?
I just want to snivel, sob, bellow, and groan.

—"I FEEL AWFUL" FROM *THE COLLECTED POEMS OF FREDDIE THE PIG* BY
WALTER R. BROOKS, AMERICAN CHILDREN'S AUTHOR

Sometimes we just want to sit, alone, with our pain and difficulty. So go ahead and sit with it—but get out your pen and paper and WRITE.

❖

* Write what you never said.
* Take some time to write down the awful stuff. The stuff you don't want to be uplifted about—don't want made pretty.
* Write about being left out.
* Write about being in the dark.
* She/he doesn't have a clue. . . .

Off the Page

Try this remarkable but simple exercise. Find a place in nature that is secluded and safe. Go out about an hour before dusk. Sit in this safe spot until darkness covers you completely. Notice all the sounds and the sights during this time. This time of day/night is considered "spiritually filled" by the Lakota tradition. Notice the feelings you have inside as the light shifts from shadow to dark. What is Spirit filling you with?

It seems only
    yesterday I used
    to believe
there was nothing
    under my skin but
    light.
If you cut me I would
    shine.
But now when I
    fall upon the
    sidewalks of life,
I skin my knees. I
    bleed.

—FROM THE POEM
"TURNING TEN" BY BILLY
COLLINS, AMERICAN POET

13

Rituals and Meditations for the Writer's Life

What makes a fire burn
is space between the logs,
a breathing space.
Too much of a good thing,
too many logs
packed in too tight
can douse the flames
almost as surely
as a pail of water would.

So building fires
requires attention
to the spaces in between,
as much as to the wood.

When we are able to build
open spaces

in the same way
we have learned
to pile on the logs,
then we can come to see how
it is fuel and absence of the fuel,
together, that make fire possible.

We only need to lay a log
lightly from time to time.

A fire
grows
simply because the space is there,
with openings
in which the flame
that knows just how it wants to burn
can find its way.

—JUDY SORUM BROWN, SPEAKER, WRITER, EDUCATOR

Breathing Space

We all need our space. Writing space. Breathing space. Private space. A space to just be alone. As a writer I need space inside of me and outside of me, and I'm guessing you do, too. Your journal is one such place. A place you can write anything and know it will be kept private (if you want). My meditation room in our home is one of my "outside of me" places. I also have a couple of places in nature I can visit for that same sense of private space.

This was not the case when I was a teenager.

I remember feeling really crowded in my teen years. The halls were always packed with teachers; friend and foe filled up my days. At home, parents, siblings, and their friends crammed the house. It wasn't until my oldest brother moved away from home that I got my own room and found enough private space. That was when I turned sixteen *and* when I began to keep journals.

A fire
grows
simply because the space is there,
with openings
in which the flame
that knows just how it wants to burn
can find its way.

You too need a place to write and to call your own. Hopefully, it is a safe space, a place where you can get away from what presses on you in your daily life and write in your journal. If you don't have one, can you find a place you can return to whenever you choose, to write, meditate, or just quietly hang out with yourself?

* Ten years from now, someone else will be living in your room (you will have moved on). Write about this person.
* Write about feeling crowded.
* Write about the home you live in now.
* Write about a favorite place.
* Write about the view out your bedroom window.

Off the Page

Where is your breathing and writing space? If you can, fill it with objects that inspire and comfort you. If that is not an option, choose an object or two to take with you when you go to that space.

Watch the movie *The Secret Garden*, based on the book by Frances Hodgson Burnett.

"For those who are interested in a spirited intimacy, listen more to the ancestors, to spirit, to the trees, to the animals. Focus on ritual. Listen to all those forces that come and speak to us that we usually ignore."

—SOBONFU E. SOMÉ,
AFRICAN SHAMAN WOMAN
FROM THE DAGARA TRIBE

Rituals and
Meditations for
the Writer's Life

Sacred Concentration

So building fires
requires attention
to the spaces in between,
as much as to the wood.

The time you put into your journal is a time of sacred concentration. So is any time you spend meditating or watching the sun rise, or praying, or reflecting on your intentions, or sitting quietly in nature. This is how you create your *inner* breathing space. If everyone were to spend ten minutes a day in sacred concentration, the world would be a friendlier place. Part of the problem is we don't take the *time* to be sacred, to hang out quietly, to concentrate on something simple but beautiful. Even our own thoughts can be beautiful. Any time you are engaged in sacred concentration you are adding to the peace and beauty within yourself and around you.

Sacred concentration through journaling, meditation, or ritual opens a deeper place in yourself that is sacred. The more you expand this sacred place within, the stronger and happier you will be on the outside. This inner sacred ground enables you to *carry your sacredness everywhere you go.* The sense of your sacredness, of having breathing space, is no longer found only when you sit down and write or meditate; it is there inside you when you are doing more ordinary things, like hanging out with friends or doing the dishes. Sacred concentration builds that inner altar of independence, confidence, and strength.

* His Holiness the fourteenth Dalai Lama was recognized by the age of four as destined to be the next Dalai Lama. Write about being born holy.
* Write about the parents of His Holiness the Dalai Lama when they discovered who their child was.
* We are all born knowing who we truly are (we may lose touch with

this later). Write from that part of you that knows who you are—who you are meant to be.

✱ "She/he was beautiful from the inside."

✱ Write about that one memory you wish you could forget.

✱ You are holy. Write about this.

◉

Meditation: Creating a Safe Inner Space

Have this read aloud slowly by someone or tape it and listen to the tape. After a few times you will be able to visit the place you imagine without being guided.

Sit in a comfortable but alert position. Have your feet firmly grounded on the floor, or lie down on the floor. Allow yourself to relax into your breathing, taking a nice deep breath through your nose and exhaling out through your mouth. Nice deep breaths . . . Again, take a nice deep breath through your nose, exhaling out through your mouth. Continue to breathe deeply like this throughout the meditation.

Imagine yourself now in a favorite place in nature. You can still feel your body in the room but your imagination is in this favorite spot. Now imagine before you a blank chalkboard. On this chalkboard is a white number "one." This "one" turns into a doorway. Visualize the details of how your doorway looks. Breathe. . . . Go up to this door and open it. You will see that this door opens up into a hallway of doors. Go ahead and step into the hallway and walk up to the first door. You will notice that the first door has above it a red light, which is on, and the sign on the door says: ALL YOUR WORRIES—DO NOT ENTER. *Breathe. . . . Now walk down to the next door. The next door also has a red light brightly shining above it and the sign reads,* COMPLAINTS—DO NOT ENTER. *You move on to the next door, which also has a red light above it and the sign reads:* SCHOOL—DO NOT ENTER. *And you go on to the next door, which is a door with a green light that shines above it. The sign on this door reads,* SAFE PLACE. *You freely open the door and enter the room, closing*

"The sun is shining— the sun is shining. That is the magic. The flowers are growing— the roots are stirring. That is the magic. Being alive is the Magic—being strong is the Magic. The Magic is in me—the Magic is in me. . . . It's in every one of us."

—MASTER COLIN IN
THE SECRET GARDEN
BY FRANCES HODGSON
BURNETT

the door behind you. Continue to breathe as you notice everything about this place; what makes up your safe place? Hang out in this place now, taking in its feeling of safety and strength. Relax or play in this place; it is your safe place to do as you please.

Give yourself two to three minutes to experience this place. And when you are ready leave the room, close and lock the door behind you. (Only you can enter this room.) Walk up the hallway, past the other doors and out the door that leads out into nature. When you are ready, feel yourself fully returned to the present, body on the chair or floor, and open your eyes.

This place is your secret place; your private place. Don't describe it to anyone (even though you may want to). This would be like giving them entrance to a very sacred and private place that you need just for yourself.

* In the privacy of your journal write about your safe place.
* Where have you not been safe?
* Write about sacred space.

Mindfulness Meditation

Sit in a comfortable yet alert position . . . holding your body in the meditative posture, like a mountain . . . alert and tall. Slowly close your eyes and begin to let go of the experiences, thoughts, and expectations you brought with you. . . . Let go . . . softening around your moods, experiences, and thoughts. Let them come . . . and let them go . . . like waves of an ocean. Allow yourself to be fully present for this practice of meditation, letting go of worries you may have been carrying with you. As you notice what's present—the thoughts that are on your mind, or the physical sensations that are rising and falling in your body—let it all come and go as it will. Get a sense of the container called "the body." Notice the physical sensations of this meditating body. Get an overall sense of this body sitting. Try not to hold on to any thoughts, but let them go. As you do this, become aware of your breathing.

Notice that in the middle of all these thoughts and feelings there is a soft sensation of breathing. Now bring your attention to this breathing. . . . Letting the breath flow by itself, notice the physical sensations of breath, the coolness of the in-breath brushing against the top of your nostrils, or the rise and fall of your belly as you breathe. Notice the physical sensation of breath as it moves in your body. Let yourself feel your life-giving breath. Rest in the breathing. Rest in the meditating body. . . .

Keep some of your awareness on the body as it continues to sit alert and tall. Be aware of this body meditating. Maintain some of your awareness on the body as you bring most of your attention to your breath. . . .

After just a few breaths you will notice that a thought carries you off on its own wave of experience and feeling. Notice where this wave of thought has taken you, let your awareness go there, then gently bring your awareness back to the breath, and to this meditating body. Rest again and again in the breath by gently focusing your attention on the physical sensations of your breath . . . letting the breath flow through you, naturally. Hold a mindful attention on your breath, noticing when your attention moves away on another wave of thought or physical sensation, returning your awareness to the sensations of your breathing and to the body meditating.

Now, when you are ready to stop meditating, gently bring your awareness to your entire body. Feel the body sitting in its upright meditative posture. . . . At this time you may gently open your eyes and refocus your attention on your environment.

Grounding Meditation

Sit in a chair with your feet uncrossed and touching the floor. Gently close your eyes and bring your awareness to your breathing. Simply notice how your body feels, without judgment; allow yourself to breathe

"Working back and forth between experience and thought, writers have more than space and time can offer. They have the whole unexplored realm of human vision."

—FROM *WRITING THE AUSTRALIAN CRAWL* BY WILLIAM STAFFORD

Rituals and Meditations for the Writer's Life

"Sacred or secular, what is the difference? If every atom inside our bodies was once a star, then it is all sacred and all secular at the same time."

—GRETEL EHRLICH, POET AND NOVELIST

naturally. Breathe . . . and notice the physical sensation of breath within your body, how it moves in and out and rises and falls in the belly. Continue to breathe while bringing your awareness down to the bottoms of your feet.

Now, continuing to breathe, imagine roots coming out from the bottoms of your feet. Visualize the roots reaching down through the floor and through the layers of the earth. Imagine this without forcing it. . . . Continue to breathe as the roots reach down deep into the Earth, to its core. Now imagine the roots pulling up core Earth energy, and that Earth energy moving up through the roots. Still breathing, bring the Earth energy up through the roots, into the bottoms of your feet, up through your legs, and into your abdomen, until it reaches your solar plexus, which is the area behind and around your belly button. Fill this area up entirely with this core Earth energy. Then imagine this energy moving back down and through the roots, into the Earth. Envision this continual circle of Earth energy coming in and going out. Sit for a few minutes in this grounded energy. Remember to breathe and to do this meditation with as little effort as possible. Trying to force our visualizations only generates more stress. No need to force and push; just imagine and breathe. . . .

Writing Is Ceremony

Writing is a form of personal ceremony, a rite directed from your very soul. At various times in your life, your mind may say "fear"; it may cause you to feel panic, but your *soul* knows the truth and will always bring you to it. The essential truth about you is that you are fundamentally courageous and curious. Staying in contact with your soul through journal writing strengthens your ability to overcome your fears. This is why giving time to your journal is in itself so precious, so very sacred. It is the ceremony of communicating with your own soul.

Your soul is constantly calling you home, home to your true

nature. Home to your natural gifts (what we often call "God-given gifts"). Your soul calls you home to everything good about yourself, and when you sit down to write in your journal, you can hear its call. Writing in your journal is also a process of releasing all the negative and harmful stuff onto the page, so it no longer interferes with your soul's intentions. This releasing is a common part of most rituals—releasing negative or outdated clutter so you can make room for the good things that presently want to get into your life. You can use your journal to let go of your fear, for example, so more confidence or more inspired ideas can come in.

Your soul *knows* there is more to life than what they portray on television—and your journal contains this "more."

- ✶ Write about wanting more.
- ✶ Write down all that clutter in your head. Write your worries, fears, and judgmental, harsh thoughts. Release them into your journal and out of your mind. Hold the intention of *releasing* yourself from these thoughts as you write them down.

Intention: The Power behind Rituals and Life

Declaring a clear intention in a ritual is key to its success. Intentions gather energy to them; therefore, what happens or does not happen in our lives often comes down to our *intentions*. Know your intention in a ritual, or in any situation for that matter, and you will bring out its potential—because *energy follows intention*. Intentions have an impact on what can happen in your life and in your ceremony. Your decision to use this book to guide you through your journal writing sets the intention of gaining independence, spiritual insight, and confidence. "Writing your way to Independence" is not only the subtitle, but also the *intention* of this book. Have you noticed yourself becoming more independent and confident as you progress through its pages? Every exercise and meditation holds an intention, and your energy follows

"You don't do a ritual just for the sake of doing a ritual. Every ritual must have a very specific purpose, a clearly stated intention. It must have something to resolve."

—SOBONFU E. SOMÉ, AFRICAN SHAMAN WOMAN FROM THE DAGARA TRIBE

this intention as you read, meditate, and write. Prayers also work this way: you request that your spiritual source help guide you with establishing and implementing your intentions.

Did you say yes to something lately? Every commitment holds an intention. Can you identify your personal intention in that agreement? Can you name the other's intention in it? The amazing thing about knowing your intentions is that you will not be too surprised by where you end up and you will be less likely to be disappointed. The truth is, however, that too many people walk through their lives NOT knowing what their intentions are—and end up in circumstances that leave them upset and confused. *Energy follows intention*, so get clear about your intentions and your life will move according to these intentions.

* What are your prayers these days? What intentions do these prayers hold? Write this all out.
* Write out a prayer for yourself. Write this prayer at the top of a journal page. Underneath this prayer, write the prayer's intention. (There may be more than one intention in this prayer.)
* Write about a time when something unexpected happened.
* How does energy follow intention? Write about this.

Off the Page

Recipe for a Ritual

Ingredients:

One or more persons
  (as needed)
Fire or candlelight
Intention
Spirits
Drums and rattles

Dance
Songs and chants
Prayer
Sage, sweet grass, or
  incense

Directions:

Before assembling ingredients, be clear with yourself about your ritual's purpose. Set your intention.

Preheat the ritual with a fire or candlelight.

Prepare the sacred container of the ritual (a circular space on the ground or floor) by cleansing with sweet grass, sage, or incense.

Take one or more people and fold in the intent of your ritual. Make sure the full purpose of your ritual is completely folded in before adding the next ingredient.

In this recipe, more cooks don't spoil the broth but improve upon it. At this time invoke all the help you can by inviting in the spiritual help necessary for this ritual.

Begin beating in the drums.

Beating drums constantly, stir in dance.

Bring mixture to a full boil.

Add in singing and chanting to taste.

Sprinkle liberally with prayer.

Simmer until the intention rises to the surface.

Reduce heat and add prayer of thanks and farewell to the spiritual helpers.

Remove from heat and let stand until mixture settles.

Goes well with change in seasons, rites of passage, transitions, and meaningful journeys of life.

Enjoy.

> "Every ritual must have a very specific purpose, a clearly stated intention. It must have something to resolve."
>
> —SOBONFU E. SOMÉ, AFRICAN WOMAN SHAMAN FROM THE DAGARA TRIBE

Empowering Your Intention

Begin by being clear about, and becoming familiar with, your intention. Take some time to consider what your life may look like once this intention is fulfilled. For example, I might ask myself, What will my life look like once my intention of living freely and com-

Keeping Your Intentions in Sight

Above my computer, where I do much of my writing, are two intentions written out on a folded piece of cardboard. This sign stands up so I can easily see it and be reminded of my present intentions. These intentions are: "I intend to live an abundant writer's life" and "I intend to live freely and compassionately." I am also aware of daily intentions and personal intentions that I have in my relationships. I write these in my journal regularly.

So choose a wish, a commitment, or a relationship in your life to write an intention for.

Victoria chose her relationship with her best friend, Sahara. Her hope is that they can be good friends once they enter their senior year and maybe they can even go off to college together. She came up with the intention: "I intend to have a lasting relationship with Sahara." I suggested that Victoria be as specific as she can with her intention—this helps direct the energy to where she wants it. So she changed the intention to: "I intend to create a good and strong friendship with Sahara."

The next step is to write out your intention in your journal in a spot where you will read it frequently, or place it somewhere in your room (on your altar if you have one) so you are reminded of it often.

Now your intention is set and ready to draw energy to it. And the more your *attention* goes to your intention, the more energy will be built into it.

passionately becomes a reality? And my answer is that I will feel kindness toward those who have offended me somehow; I will have the ability to not be concerned about opinions others have of me. Forming a clear picture of how your life will look with the intention fulfilled makes it easier for you to know how well you are following your intention at any given time.

Once you are clear about your intention, write out a ritual for empowering that intention. Like a story, a ritual has a beginning, a middle, and an end. You begin your ritual by deciding what spiritual sources you are going to call into your ritual, and who is going to be part of your ritual, if anyone. For the middle of the ritual, you need to decide how you will "act out" its intention. If the intention of your ritual is to create happiness in a particular area in your life, how will you show this in your ceremony? In many ways this part of the ritual is like a play you are performing with the spirit world, calling on their help and showing them what your prayer, your intention, is. To complete your ceremony, you will give your spiritual sources some demonstration of gratitude and release them back to their world.

✶ As a creative writing exercise, write in your journal about planning and performing a ritual and about what happens in your life afterward.

Off the Page

Now ask yourself, am I ready to perform a ritual so that my intention can be sent out to the world? For more about rituals, please check out my book *The Thundering Years: Rituals and Sacred Wisdom for Teens*.

Claiming Your Own Story

Every moment of your life is part of your unfolding story. One of the values of journal writing is that journals provide a keepsake of *your* life story. Later, it will help you to remember certain events if you decide to use them in a novel or memoir, or even tell them as anecdotes in a presentation (or a roast!). Mostly it is a way to claim your life and all its stories as your own; the way *you* experienced and remember them. Your brothers and sisters may have grown up in

"There are many circles in life. . . . With this first circle, you will start the first step in finding your path, the first step in finding yourself. Remember, do not get caught on just one circle; if you do, you will forever be going around in circles. Grasp the knowledge of that circle and then move on to the next. One day you will look up, and you will be at the center, and the mystery of life will be revealed to you."

—Wa'Na'Nee'Che' (Dennis Renault), Native American teacher and civil rights attorney

Rituals and Meditations for the Writer's Life

237

the same household as you, but I can guarantee that your stories and memories are unique. Listen to, trust, and write your own stories.

This story is from the book *Winona's Web: A Novel of Discovery* by Priscilla Cogan.*

I'm a pipe carrier for my people. Ours is the way of this land. The land of Jesus was dry, stony, desert country. His is the story from that place. Ours is the way of the buffalo people. The black robes came to my people and told them the stories of Jesus. We said they were fine stories, now let us tell you our stories. We said let us tell you how this turtle continent was made, how fire came to the buffalo people, the lessons of the coyote. We said let us tell you of the pipe and the seven ceremonies brought to us by White Buffalo Calf Woman. But they were rude people, these black robes. They wanted us to hear only their stories. They said their stories were the true stories. And then the elders knew how foolish these black robes were, for no one story could tell it all, and all stories are true.

* Who is unwilling to listen to your stories?
* What ancient stories exist in the area where you live? What native tribes lived where you now live? Read and write about that.
* Write a story about something that happened to you recently. Write it as if you are telling a story about someone else.
* Write about being rude.
* *Winona's Web* is autobiographical fiction—the author borrows from her life but also invents some parts here and there. Write a scene or a short story that borrows from your life, adding some fictional material.

Off the Page

Contact your grandparents or great grandparents if they are alive. Collect at least one story from them and write it down in your journal. How does this story influence your life?

*Published by Main Street Books, New York, 1997.

"Things are not untrue just because they never happened."

—DENNIS HAMLEY, ENGLISH CHILDREN'S AUTHOR

Rituals and Meditations for the Writer's Life

14

The Afterlife

I arise each day
Through the strength of heaven:
Light of sun,
Radiance of moon,
Splendor of fire,
Speed of lightning,
Swiftness of wind,
Depth of sea,
Stability of earth,
Firmness of rock.

—Irish song attributed to Saint Patrick

"Be at peace with your own soul, then heaven and earth will be
at peace with you. Enter eagerly into the treasure house that
is within you, and you will see the things that are in heaven; for
there is but one single entry to them both. The Ladder that leads
to the Kingdom is hidden within your soul. . . . Dive into yourself,
and in your soul you will discover the stairs by which to ascend."

—Saint Isaac of Nineveh

The Big Questions

A lot of people try to tell us what to believe about the afterlife, about God, about who to listen to and who *not* to listen to; and about how to interpret such holy texts as the Bible or Koran. There have been times I was afraid to ask the Big Questions, mostly afraid of what "the" answer might be. In reality, looking back I see that asking and living these questions (even though it was painful at times) is what made me strong. These questions nourished a life of curiosity and inner independence, as well as a deep connection to Spirit.

Some people don't want you to question their version of the truth; their interpretation of holy text. Why is that? Some people don't want you to consider anything but what they say is right. There are thousands of interpretations of the Christian Bible. How is this so? Which one is the correct one? Treck, an eighteen-year-old from Sweden, says it best: "How is it the Creator gave us a mind to consider all the possibilities and would not want us to figure these things out for ourselves?"

Wouldn't it be more gracious, and even more sacred, for the clergy of all faiths to allow each one of us to consider the big questions of life for ourselves? Why am I here? Where is God? Is there a God? What do I think of Jesus' teachings? What is karma? Do I believe in sin? Why would God send anyone that he loved to hell? What happens when we die? Do I believe in reincarnation?

You have heard it is not the destination but the journey that truly matters. This is so of life and applies to all the big questions as well. Perhaps God (the Creator, Yaweh, Spirit, etc.) just wants you to keep asking the big questions—to go into each moment wondering what it might all be about. And from this open heart and mind, you will find answers. Something will come into your open, questioning heart that will make sense to you. Give it time. And never give up. Continue to ask the questions, and the answers will come to you naturally and certainly. In those moments of clarity, leave room for the mystery and for the next question. . . .

I was sixteen and my aunt invited me to go to Florida with her, my uncle, and my six-year-old cousin. I was to babysit my cousin. I left my boyfriend and my family back home. At the time, I was struggling—with high school, a father who was gone a lot, a brother with schizophrenia, and a boyfriend who was addicted to pot. Since the age of seven I had been actively in search of God—of the meaning of life, of where I belonged in the Big Picture . . . and my need for answers was very intense that spring as I headed to Florida with my relatives.

I usually found myself in church on Easter Sunday, which fell during spring break that year. This time, wearing short shorts and a sleeveless tee shirt, I sat in the back of a Southern Baptist church. My heart beat hard and fast when I heard the sermon. The minister wailed on about the blood of Christ and about sinners and eternity. . . . Then he asked if anyone was ready to "accept Jesus into their heart." Oh yes, I was—but every time I had said yes to this I never *felt* anything happen in my heart. So I sat quietly, heart pounding hard because a lot of what he was saying was upsetting me.

At the end of the sermon he greeted everyone as they walked out. I shook his hand and boldly said that I didn't agree that Jesus' main message was about blood and sin; he meant for us to love one another, he taught us about tolerance and forgiveness (I had studied the Bible myself by then). He looked at me sternly and said, "You, my girl, are going to hell." He then turned his back to me.

Very upset, I walked past the others he was greeting and tried not to cry. An older woman, an elder of the church, approached me. "Don't worry dear. It will be okay. He's this way because he talks to God every day." I went back to the hotel, head pounding with questions. *Was I going to hell? Does this man really have conversations with God? Am I on the wrong path? Why don't I actually feel Jesus in my heart?* I journaled all this into my small travel diary. The next day, I set out for the church. The door was open so I just walked in. I stayed in there for hours, praying for help. Praying to feel Jesus in my heart. Then the elder who had spoken to me the previous day came in and I asked her if I could see the minister—I had some questions for him. She told me his house was next door on the same lot as the church, and that he had some time for me after lunch.

I spent a few hours with him. He mostly answered my questions by telling me what was right and what was wrong. Like why people shouldn't dance together before they marry. I left, heart and head still pounding. The elder and I exchanged addresses and on my return home we began a yearlong correspondence.

"A rabbi whose congregation does not want to drive him out of town isn't a rabbi."

—Talmudic saying

The Afterlife

241

I would write to her about my concerns, my life, and my spiritual questions. She would recommend books to read, and Bible verses to study.

I was in a lot of pain. I was ending my two-year relationship with my boyfriend, my brother was getting sicker, and my father was even more absent. I kept reading and writing. Then one day the following spring, when my brother was having a particularly hard time, I decided to write to the minister for help. After all, with his direct contact with God he could surely help me. I wrote him a letter and put it into the letter to the elder. I asked, since he holds council with God every day, could he please ask Him to help my brother and my father. I was entirely sincere and hopeful. It felt like a last chance. I poured my heart out.

A week later an envelope stuffed with a large letter came to me. I opened it up, to find another letter from the elder. Not one word from the minister. She answered my letter to him with more biblical quotes and suggested verses. I took the letter out to the backyard, which was at one time an apple orchard. I looked up into the big blue sky and held my own conversation with God. I said, "If this is his response, then he is not my link to you, or to the truth. There is something wrong here, God, if he can't respond honestly to me. I trust you are up there somewhere, and I guess I will have to go it alone with you for now." I never wrote again, and the elder never sent me another letter either.

—AUTHOR'S JOURNAL

* Make a list of your big questions.
* Write about a church or synagogue, or describe a religious experience of any kind.
* Write about an encounter with a religious elder.
* Is anyone trying to make you believe something that does not feel right to you at this time? Write about this.
* Write about limbo.

What Do You Really Believe?

I grew up with the general knowledge of God and Christianity, but my mother, being a single lesbian mother, never attended church. I had my questions, so when I was seven or eight my mom gave me a copy of the Bible. I read the whole thing through but found myself asking more questions having not found any answers. I guess I should say that I never felt belief for anything I read; to me it didn't make any sense. For several years after this I hovered in a cloud of wanting to believe something, but unable to find what it was that I truly believed in.

When I went into junior high I discovered witchcraft, or rather Hollywood's version of witchcraft. As I began to look deeper and read the true history of the witch trials I found myself becoming more and more fascinated with real life witchcraft—Wicca. The more books I read, the more I felt a connection, finally, to something that made much more sense in my mind. Karma, spirit, whatever you want to call it, made sense to me and left me with no unanswered questions.

The only religious figures I'd ever known in my life were the ones on TV. That is, I guess I had to be my own spiritual advisor. I told myself to remain open-minded, that my beliefs weren't everyone else's. Conflicting beliefs and religious viewpoints ruined several friendships throughout my years in school. I know now, having been a solitary practitioner for over seven years, that I have found my niche in the religious world.

To me, death is the passing on of our personalities from the physical form to the boundary-free pure energy form. I don't believe in the golden gates welcoming you into heaven if you've lived your life according to God's rules, or being cast into a pit of fire if you've failed those rules in any way. Moreover, I also believe in reincarnation—I believe it was Albert Einstein who proved that energy is neither created nor destroyed, but continuous. You can feel a person's energy when they enter a room, when they shake your hand, when you look a person straight in the eyes . . . you can feel your lover's presence. This is the energy I speak of that passes along when we die. So in a sense we never really die, just pass on. That's my belief.

—JADE DYE, AGE 19, WRITER

In the middle of my freshman year of high school my mom decided we were going to move with her fiancé across the river to Iowa. My mom got married the next fall.

As time went on she started going to church with my stepfather, Robert.

This was a strange thing to me because I had been told all through my life that religion had no point and that going to church was a waste of time. I became confused as to what to believe.

I didn't want to go to church at first but eventually I did start to go more often. I started to question a lot of things in life—especially about religion/faith/spirituality.

I met some friendly people at church, which made the whole thing seem welcoming. But I still had questions nagging in the back of my head, and still do. I've tried for a couple of years now to get some of those questions answered by taking classes and participating in church youth groups. I feel like the girl in the story—I keep wanting to accept God, but I never quite feel connected.

This frustrates me so much. I feel like I need some sort of spiritual connection, but I can't seem to grasp it. Why?

Sometimes I feel like learning about God has been worse for me than not being connected. Before, I was happy with my life. Now I feel that the Christian religion almost makes me feel worse at times because I sin or do things wrong, but I don't know how to feel forgiven. Other times I feel good about the religion, when I know how much that community of people cares. I just feel like my mind bounces back and forth all the time and I can't settle on something.

It's hard for me to think that there is some sort of god out there. I think of it more as a spirit of our whole universe that we are all connected to in some way. In the back of my mind I think I know that all the questions I have can never be answered for certain. But I hate not understanding something, it irritates me. Maybe I have been struggling with this more than I think I have, and maybe I haven't tried hard enough either.

One thing I question especially is: How do I know which religion is the "right" one? I know Christians often believe that they are on the right path and they want to save all others. But what about all the other religions out there? Do they not count? How do I ever truly believe in one religion when there are so many out there? I just can't say that one is right over another.

—AMANDA, AGE 18

* What would you like the truth to be about God, Spirit, the afterlife? Write this in your journal.
* Write about your greatest fear at this time in regards to the Big Questions.

The Happily Ever After Life

"A fish said to another fish, 'Above this sea of ours there
is another sea, with creatures swimming in it—
and they live there even as we live here.'
"The fish replied, 'Pure fancy! Pure fancy! When you know that everything that leaves our sea by even an inch, and stays out of it, dies.
What proof have you of other lives in other seas?' "

—FROM *THE PROPHET* BY KAHLIL GIBRAN,
LEBANESE POET AND MYSTIC

"Life is not separate
from death. It only
looks that way."

—BLACKFOOT SAYING

My idea of the afterlife has changed, and may continue to change.
Buddhists believe that in the afterlife you go through a series of
"bardo" states (states of consciousness), and then you may be reincar-
nated. Many Christians believe in a Judgment Day when you appear
before God and he decides whether you enter heaven or hell. Taoists
believe you become part of the great Tao, part of everything. Many
Native Americans believe you become part of the spirit world.

A Lutheran pastor asked Jessica's confirmation group, "Where do
you think you go when you die?" Jessica, who is thirteen, responded:
"It is our own little sanctuary, a place of importance to us. I hope it
will be a place near the ocean, with a beautiful cottage. . . ."

In Alice Sebold's novel *The Lovely Bones,* a young woman who is
murdered experiences the afterlife as a movement from one stage of
heaven to another, where she is able to watch some of the goings-on
in the world below. Another bestseller, *The Five People You Meet in
Heaven* by Mitch Albom, tells about one man's encounters in heaven
with five significant people he knew in his lifetime. In both books
the main characters get to work through some unresolved issues
before moving on to the final place—which of course remains a
mystery. These books give the reader the idea that maybe we create
our own version of heaven through what we believe and imagine
heaven to be. This mirrors the viewpoint of the recent movie *What
Dreams May Come,* in which everyone ends up in their version of

the afterlife, with options to return to Earth or remain in heaven. The possibility that we may be partly responsible for what kind of afterlife we experience fascinates me. We certainly are responsible for what kind of life we experience.

> "This is a story about a man named Eddie and it begins at the end, with Eddie dying in the sun. It might seem strange to start a story with an ending. But all endings are also beginnings. We just don't know it at the time."
>
> —OPENING OF *THE FIVE PEOPLE YOU MEET IN HEAVEN* BY MITCH ALBOM

* Who are the five people you might meet in heaven?
* What would you consider to be an ideal afterlife?
* What, if anything, have you been told comes after life? Does this feel right to you?
* Describe dying, using images from nature.

FIREFLIES
I got caught up
in the last remaining fireflies of the summer twilight . . .
shadows of gold
slanting across feather-tipped grasses
crickets chirping
on their low-hanging eaves
i hear the drums
pounding an ancient rhythm
echoing throughout the air around me

birds take flight
animals burrow underneath
their woodland homes
drums

"There is no death, only a change of worlds."

—DUWAMISH WISDOM

The Afterlife

the essence of authority
bending their beat
only to the fireflies

—JOY RANDOLPH, AGE 21

Packing for the Big Trip

Today four local teen boys died in a car accident. Two were brothers and all were from the same rural town. Grief counselors went to the school to help those who knew the boys. What to do in the face of such loss? When such a tragedy occurs, something so painful happens close to home (not overseas or to some stranger mentioned on the late news), then *we know*. We know that we are all fragile. We realize that death can come at any moment.

I think of death as a trip we are all going on but few are packing for. We need to allow the reality of loss and death to enter our consciousness. I don't mean to make death what we live for, or to be constantly thinking of death, but to not be avoiding it either. Since it is a trip we are all going on, it would be good to have a suitcase ready for when the time comes. By this I mean a spiritual suitcase, a metaphorical suitcase. In it is what we need to have a good passing from this life to the next. Again it is very important not to carry this suitcase around with you all the time—but to have it safely packed at home. Death is inevitable but LIFE is what calls to you now.

So what would be in your spiritual suitcase? In my suitcase is my Guru Padmasambhava, and his mantra (om ah hung benza guru pema sidhi hum) that I intend to recite as I pass from this life into the next. All those I love are there in my suitcase, smiling at me, wishing me a great journey. The silence and the ability to sit in silence are there in my suitcase. I've also included some letters and reminders from loved ones and others telling me of the good impact I had on them in this lifetime. There are no regrets in my suitcase. And there is the knowledge that everything is connected to everything

"Dying is part of the wheel, right there next to being born. . . . Being part of the whole thing, that's the blessing."

—FROM *TUCK EVERLASTING* BY NATALIE BABBITT, CHILDREN'S FANTASY AUTHOR

The Afterlife

247

else, which makes me unafraid. All this is in my imaginary (yet very real) spiritual suitcase.

Jesus is in my suitcase and his teachings on love and forgiveness. The LIGHT that I can connect with in my heart, and the hope. I see beauty even when all is bleak and black. All the people I love; those who have held me through difficult times, warming me with their love and possibilities. The Creator is in there—connecting me to everything and everyone. All these things help me remember about eternal love. The light and love that connects us all holds my hand.

—DANIELLE, AGE 19

* Write about what is in your suitcase. What will help you in your own journey? These are the same things that will help you deal with the loss of a loved one as well.
* Write about a loss you have had.
* Write about tomorrow.

The Death of a Teacup

—from The Wisdom of the Crows and Other Buddhist Tales, retold by Sherab Choddzin and Alexandra Kohn

There once was a great teacher of Zen, a school of the Buddha's teachings that is very down to earth about how things in life really are. This great teacher's name was Ikkyu. Even as a young boy he was very clever and always found a way of getting himself out of trouble.

One day as he was playing, Ikkyu knocked over a teacup, which fell to the floor and shattered into pieces. Now the teacup belonged to his teacher, and it was very old and precious, and his teacher valued it greatly. As Ikkyu was worrying about this accident, he heard his teacher coming and quickly hid the pieces of the cup behind his back. When his teacher appeared, Ikkyu asked him, "Why do people die?"

"That is just natural," his teacher replied. "Everything only has so long to live, and then it must die."

At these words, Ikkyu showed his teacher the pieces of the broken teacup.

Born Again and Again

"I don't know when I'll be back.
But back I will be."

—**WILLIAM STEIG, AUTHOR AND ILLUSTRATOR OF CHILDREN'S BOOKS**

I am asked all the time if I believe in reincarnation, or if I can do past-life readings on people. Mostly my answer is—it depends on the day you ask me. I find it is always fun to be open to the possibility of past lives, and future stories.

I have these repetitive dreams of an Atlantis-like place. I know this place very well and have relationships and adventures there. I have a clear picture of it in my mind and I often miss it when I awake. A lot happens there. So, for me it doesn't really matter whether or not it is real in a way that can be proven. It is real to me in the same way that stories are real, or that any memory is real. Once something is over, done, it becomes a memory, a dream, a story. Real in one's memory, but not real (actual) in the moment.

Past-Life Meditation

You are going to take a journey to your past, to one of your past lives. Again, it does not matter if you are certain about past lives or not—trust what comes, and write about it in your journal. Have this read out loud to you by a friend, counselor, or spiritual teacher. Give yourself five minutes for this meditation and then five more to write down your experiences and response to the journey.

Perhaps the earth can teach us
as when everything
seems to be dead
in winter
and later proves to be alive.

—**PABLO NERUDA, CHILEAN POET**

The Afterlife

Lie down on the floor or sit comfortably in a chair. Find your breath. . . . Now take ten deep breaths, and on the exhales try to expel all the air. Let your body fill up with the breath, and then empty out the breath completely. Then relax on the floor. Feel your body relax, every muscle loosening, the mind relaxing and letting go. Feel the rise and fall of the breath and relax into it. . . . Now imagine yourself in a place in nature that you enjoy.

There is a cave entrance nearby, or some opening into the earth. This opening can be a place you have actually visited if one comes to mind. Bring this place into focus and rest your full attention on this image of the cave entrance. The opening goes down deep into the earth, where there are many caverns and rooms. The opening should feel both familiar and comfortable to you.

Slowly approach the entrance to the cave and enter the opening. Notice the smells of the rich earth, the stillness of the tunnel, the feel of your body as it enters this place. Just inside the entrance of the cave, you will meet a spirit guardian that will help you on your journey. It may come in the form of an animal, a guardian angel, an ancestor, a ball of energy, a person, or a voice. This being will be your spirit guide on your shamanic journey.

Ask your guide to show you a past life. Your guide will then lead you down a tunnel into the underworld. This passage is usually short, ending in a room or a place in nature. Your guide has taken you to a place where you will find the answer to your question. Trust whatever comes. Just go with the experience and keep focused on the journey. You want to be present for whatever happens on the journey.

When you feel that the journey is done, bring yourself back to the place where you entered the underworld. Thank your guide and come back through the tunnel and out of the cave opening. Don't bring anything back with you from your journey that you didn't take in with you.

Then feel yourself in your body and back in the room, on the floor, breathing. Take some time to reacquaint yourself with the room.

* Now write in your journal about this past-life experience.
* How is this past life linked to your present life?
* Write about unfinished business.

Saying Good-bye to Stoney

—by Karen Braun, Horse Medicine Woman, animal healer, writer

Stoney, our twenty-eight-year-old quarter horse was a deep red chestnut with a wide white blaze running the whole length of his face. We called him "Grampa." He had arthritis and moved slowly and stiffly. He was the kind of horse we could just let loose on our front lawn for hours to graze. We'd look out the window every now and then to see that he'd only moved about ten feet, eating every blade of grass around him. He was the kind of horse always to be trusted. He loved children and cats.

He developed a serious disease called Cushing's Disease. It had many symptoms, one of which was laminitis in his feet (a very painful and sometimes irreversible problem). In the space of a few days he could barely walk. The vet pretty much told us to say our good-byes one Saturday. There was nothing left to do to help him. How does one do that . . . say good-bye to a beloved horse, a trusted friend? We made plans with the vet to come back Monday morning to put "Grampa" down.

Sunday morning Stoney was a bit brighter. He carefully ambled his way over to the grassy paddock to eat. I spent the day with him, loving him, catering to his every need. It was a gorgeous fall day. By early evening though, things changed dramatically. I sat on the ground next to him as he stood there shuffling his weight back and forth on all feet trying to relieve the pressure and pain. I believe he chose not to lie down because he knew he couldn't get back up. I sobbed into his furry neck for more than an hour. His breathing was shallow and labored. The light in his huge brown eyes had gone out. We were in his stall and I told him that I would call the vet to come now to set him free instead of

" 'I don't think I'll last forever,' said Peach. 'That's okay,' said Blue, 'Not many folks do. 'But until then, you have me, and I have you.' "

—FROM *PEACH AND BLUE* BY SARAH S. KILBORNE, AUTHOR AND ILLUSTRATOR

waiting until tomorrow as planned. I went in the house to make the call.

I came back outside twenty minutes later to find Stoney not only out of his stall, but standing at the other end of the paddock in the exact spot that I wanted him to be in for his transition! I was shocked! For a horse who couldn't walk, he'd managed to get to that spot all on his own! He knew he was moments away from freedom. I waited with him for the vet to arrive with the euthanasia solution. I told Stoney how much I loved him, and he willingly took one more carrot from me and ate the whole thing! The vet lovingly administered the shot, and Stoney, our dear Grampa, fell to the earth where we had him buried. After it was done, my crying, anxiety, and hysterics simply stopped. I was so relieved to have helped set his spirit free from his pain-filled body. It was the last act of real love I could give him . . . letting him go. We now call his burial spot "Stoney's paddock." The grass grows lushly there.

- ✱ Write about what pets bring to our lives.
- ✱ Have you lost a pet? Write your story of letting go.
- ✱ What does it really mean to let go?
- ✱ Write a letter to yourself from your pet.

Staying Connected

> "They are not dead who live in the hearts they leave behind."
>
> —**TUSCARORA PROVERB**

When my father died I put together a special journal and picture album. It included poetry I wrote about my father, pictures of my father and me, some journal entries, and a prayer. Here is a poem I wrote into the album after he died.

MY FAVORITE MEMORY

He would fill the doorway with his football player body,

pockets filled with miniature toys,

"We die, and we do not die."

—**SHUNRYU SUZUKI,**
ZEN MASTER,
JAPANESE AUTHOR

shrunk to size, This is what I remember
about Friday nights when my father returned home from long absences.
He lived in his car during the week selling paper products
to people across Wisconsin.
How I loved his many deep, safe and abundant pockets.
A time for me to get greedy and grabby and happy with him,
searching for me on his trips.

Time took a lot of this memory
I don't remember what the toys were—
or how many times he actually filled the doorway.

He stopped filling up doorways once he became small with cancer.

But there was a time when my father filled up doorways
and we hung out together in a place that never dies.

On Father's Day I write in the blank pages that are left in the back of the photo journal. It is a way for me to visit my father and to remember him. (He was cremated, so there is no grave to visit.)

If a best friend is moving away, together you can take some time to put together an album. Make sure to leave some blank pages in the back of the journal to write in on his or her birthday.

* Write about a favorite memory with your father.
* Write about doorways.
* Write about seeing someone for the last time.

The Afterlife

The Afterlife

254

Off the Page

When someone you love dies, put together a photo journal to remember them. Or you may want to begin a photo album of your parents or other loved ones now.

What you will need:

a blank photo journal or a journal with unlined pages

photos of your loved one

your journals

Allow a few hours to gather pictures, poems, letters, and journal entries. Arrange them in the journal, leaving as much as half of the pages blank to add more photos, poetry, or prose later.

Creating A Grief Ritual

Our culture teaches us to suppress our grief (and even our joy). In order to grieve properly, you must grieve with others. It is not enough to cry alone in your room. It is definitely not enough to go on as if nothing has happened.

Communal expression of grief releases immeasurable pain that the individuals present have never truly released. I have gone through grief rituals with Sobonfu and Malidoma Somé of the Dagara tribe of Africa and have found great relief and healing in communal grieving. It will open you up in a way that no other process can. It has the power to heal physical, mental, spiritual, and social wounds. Grieving frees the past, the ancestors, the sufferings—and each of us, as well. Without the release of grief, our community and our individual psyches remain stuck.

In the story *The Secret Garden* it is through a small ritual that a child learns to release her pent-up sorrow. She had lost both her parents yet she did not cry until the ritual was complete. Many of us carry around with us hurts, losses, and disappointments that can be freed only through the expression of our grief. In the Dagara tradition they believe that we also carry in us the unexpressed pain of our ancestors. So, you not only grieve to heal yourself, you grieve to heal everyone.

You can get together with your friends, your family and others who cared about someone who died and practice your own grief ritual. First take the time to write out how you would like the ritual to look. Use your journal to record all your ideas.

Below are some ideas about what to include in your grief ritual. The rest is up to you. Give yourself at least half an hour to write down your ritual.

What would you like to express about this person?

How is this loss like all losses?

How can your ritual create a safe space for everyone to have their feelings expressed?

What needs to be blessed?

What needs to be released?

What needs to be said or sung?

Dagara Grief Ritual

This ritual should be led by someone who is experienced with such processes. This can be a transpersonal psychotherapist, a ritual facilitator, or a skillful shaman like Sobonfu Somé.

As in all rituals, this one has a beginning, which is the invoking of spiritual sources; a middle, acting out the intent of the ritual; and an ending, giving thanks to those spiritual sources that helped in the ritual. There is a designated place to weep, to wail, to grieve out loud. This is called a grieving or wailing circle. At least twenty feet away is a grieving altar. On this altar photos of the deceased and spiritually significant objects are placed. Some people will bring an item that represents the deceased. At one ceremony a woman brought a note her father wrote to her; at another a woman brought a bag of M&Ms, her friend's favorite treat.

To begin, the area is smudged with sage and everyone gathers

The Afterlife

255

in the grieving circle. They take time to invoke the help of everyone's spiritual sources (out loud) and invite in those they will be grieving, calling their names out loud. (I always face each compass direction and call in the guardians and energies of each direction.) Then the facilitator/shaman begins to read poems and stories aloud that invoke the emotions of sadness, loss, and grief. Music is often played as well.

When the readings are finished, everyone grieves aloud, crying, breathing, weeping in a circle together for as long as they need to. Then when each person feels it is his or her time, one by one they will make the journey from the wailing circle to the grieving altar, voicing their grief and weeping all the way. Each mourner then makes an offering of their grief at the altar, just as a sacred object may be placed on an altar as an offering. The grief is offered for the loved one who has died, and for anyone who has not been grieved.

In the Dagara tradition, it is understood that many, many deaths and losses have not been grieved, so as a community we carry this pain in our psyches. This pain needs to be released, and the many departed who have not been grieved need our tears and acknowledgment so they can heal and move on. This is core to the Dagara ritual and philosophy. They are the ones who say, "When someone has died it is NOT business as usual." Think of all the people throughout time who have not been wept over. The earth and our souls carry this—and with our tears and acknowledgment we release it from ourselves and from the earth.

Once people finish offering their grief at the altar, they step to the side and wait for the rest to take their turns until everyone has made the journey from the grieving circle to the altar. The group then sings songs or chants of gratitude, of peace, and of love. The ceremony ends with everyone thanking the spirits who have come to the ritual, releasing them from this place.

Consider having an altar where you can put the loved one's photo and other objects that represent this person. You may want to include other spiritual objects, offerings to the ancestors—any objects that represent what you are grieving.

You can use birdseed in your ceremony. In many traditions birds are believed to carry our dead, our grief, and our songs to the spirit world.

Many traditions feast, and even celebrate the person's life, once the grieving period is done. What would you like included in your feast (perhaps the deceased's favorite food)?

* Create your own grief ritual for someone who has passed, first writing it out in your journal.
* Make a list of at least six people who would be interested in holding this ritual with you.

Off the Page

Check out my Web site: julietallardjohnson.com for links to those who perform grief rituals.

"People who do not know how to weep together are people who cannot laugh together. People who know not the power of shedding their tears together are like a time bomb, dangerous to themselves and to the world around them. The Dagara understand the expression of emotion as a process of self-kindling or calming, which not only helps in handling death but also resets or repairs the feelings within the person."

—MALIDOMA PATRICE SOMÉ, AFRICAN SHAMAN AND AUTHOR

"The kingdom of heaven is like treasure hidden in a field, which a man found and covered up; then in his joy he goes and sells all that he has and buys that field."

—GOSPEL OF MATTHEW 13:44

The Afterlife

15

Going Off the Page

"If we all did the things we are capable of doing,
we would literally astound ourselves."

—Thomas Edison, American inventor

"There is no use in trying," said Alice. "I cannot believe
impossible things." "I dare say you haven't had much
practice," said the Queen. "When I was your age, I always
did it for half an hour a day. Why, sometimes I've believed
as many as six impossible things before breakfast."

—from *Alice in Wonderland* by Lewis Carroll

Thunder Wisdom

My hope for you when you are upset with the world around you is that you take time to listen with your heart for what you believe to be true—and, with courage, write and speak this truth. I say this because your community (both the local community and the global one) needs to hear your voice—the voice of our young adults.

What do you need to speak out about? What are your concerns in your personal life, in your community, in the world around you? What do you witness that upsets you? What do you sense would make the adults in your life uneasy if you *did* speak out about it? What needs to be talked about—and heard? What are you passionate about? What moves you to compassionate action?

What is your truth?

The "truth" that you need to express is part of the "Thunder Wisdom" you hold during the Thundering Years—your teenage and young adult years. This energy and wisdom is a powerful force that you can use to help those who are suffering and in need, including yourself and the planet. Compassionate action is "acting out" with purpose. It is using your Thunder energy in a powerful and positive way. It is the thunder in the storm that brings the rain to feed the soil and plants. The thunder may frighten us because it is so noisy, but it brings us needed nourishment. Bring us—your community—what we need. Let us hear your thunder.

Your emotions may be many and intense: sadness, confusion, numbness, hope, hopelessness, fear, and anger. We are not typically encouraged to listen to our anger. Instead, we are instructed to "control" it. While it is important not to harm anyone with our anger, the emotion itself is valuable. It's worth paying attention to and doing something with. Your intensity is an important part of who you are right now. And your anger, along with your need to "act out," is also a part of this intensity. Getting your message heard can be a challenge. Speaking out about your feelings, protesting issues that concern you, expressing your anger *creatively,* and helping others speak out are

"We are here because there are things that need our help. Like the planet. Like each other. Like animals. The world is like a garden, and we are its protectors."

—B. B. KING,
BLUES MUSICIAN

Going Off the Page

powerful ways to use your energy. Acting out with what wisdom-keepers refer to as "skillful means"—rocking the boat without harming anyone—is part of the intense journey into independence.

Anger can be an invitation to take a new road—or to make a new road—because something is not working the old way.

Start Where You Are

It's easy to get overwhelmed with the enormity and complexity of things you'd like to see done differently in the world. Before you get paralyzed into no action at all, *stop* . . . take a breath . . . and think of what you might do if you could change *one* thing. Keep it small. Keep it simple. It doesn't need to be big to make a big difference. None of us has to look very far to know we are needed.

Just look around—where there is pain, there is a need for help. Or look inside yourself. You may choose to help others whose suffering is similar in nature or cause to your own. Simply being kind to someone can generate a lot of healing, both in that person and in yourself.

Don't be afraid to reach out, speak up, and help yourself and others. As Mahatma Gandhi said, "We must be the change we want in the world." I believe your young adult years are of great importance for you and for the community. I know you hold a lot of vision and opinions about the world—your school, the violence around us, what might help, what is going wrong, and what we could do better. Please let your voice be heard.

Send a letter to the local paper, make a poster or a bumper sticker, write a poem, speak up to others, pray for those who are hurting. Volunteer your time and energy, listen to someone, smile at a stranger, finish some project, seek help in ending abuse in your life, call your grandparents, sit down and have a meal with your family, read a book to someone who can't read, learn to meditate, send a letter to someone, go for a walk to contemplate what is truly beautiful about this planet. You will feel better, much better, and you will help countless people—people you care about, and people you will never meet.

> "The best possible work has not yet been done. If I were twenty-one today I would elect to join the communicating network of those young people, the world over, who recognize the urgency of life-supporting change, knowledge joined to action: knowledge about what man has been and is can protect the future."
>
> **—Margaret Mead, American anthropologist**

> "I don't know what your destiny will be, but one thing I know: the only ones among you who will be really happy are those who have sought and found how to serve."
>
> **—Dr. Albert Schweitzer, theologian, philosopher, and musician**

> *May your life be like a*
> *wildflower,*
> *growing freely in the*
> *beauty*
> *and joy of each day.*
>
> **—Native American proverb**

Small service is true
    service. . .
The daisy, by the
    shadow that it
    casts,
Protects the lingering
    dewdrop from the
    sun.

—William Wordsworth, English poet

Selected Bibliography

The Art of Drowning by Billy Collins, University of Pittsburgh Press, 1995.

Awakening The Buddhist Heart by Lama Surya Das, Broadway Books, 2000.

Butterflies in the Mud by Lia Joy Rundle, 2000. Chapbook available at Julietallardjohnson.com

The Collected Poems of Charles Olson edited by George F. Butterick, University of California Press, 1987.

Coloring Mandalas for Insight, Healing and Self-Expression by Susanne F. Fincher, Shambhala, 2000.

A Creative Writer's Kit: A Spirited Companion and Lively Muse for the Writing Life by Judy Reeves, New World Library, 2003.

A Drifting Boat: An Anthology of Chinese Zen Poetry edited by Seaton and Dennis Maloney, White Pine Press, 1994.

The Enlightened Heart: An Anthology of Sacred Poetry edited by Stephen Mitchell, HarperPerennial, 1989.

The Essential Rumi, translations by Coleman Marks with John Moyne, HarperSanFrancisco, 1995.

Finding What You Didn't Lose: Expressing Your Truth and Creativity Through Poetry by John Fox, Putnam Books, 1995.

The Hidden Messages of Water by Masaru Emoto, translated by David A. Thayne, Beyond Words Publishing, 2004.

A Hidden Wholeness: The Journey Toward an Undivided Life by Parker J. Palmer, Jossey-Bass, 2004.

The House on Mango Street by Sandra Cisneros, Vintage Books, 1991.

How to Think Like Leonardo da Vinci: Seven Steps to Genius Every Day by Michael J. Gelb, Random House, 1998.

The I Ching or Book of Changes by Brian Browne Walker, St Martin's Griffin, 1992.

If You Want to Write by Brenda Ueland, The Schubert Club, 1983.

The Inferno by Dante Alighieri, Signet Classics, 2001.

Issa: Cup-of-Tea Poems by David G. Lanoue, Asian Humanities Press, 1991.

Leaves of Grass by Walt Whitman, Bantam Classics, 1983.

Letters from a Wild State: Rediscovering Our True Relationship to Nature by James G. Cowan, Bell Tower, 1991.

The Lie That Tells the Truth: A Guide to Writing Fiction by John Dufresne, W.W. Norton & Company, 2003.

News of the Universe: Poems of Twofold Consciousness chosen and introduced by Robert Bly, Sierra Club Books, 1980.

The Observation Deck: A Tool Kit for Writers by Naomi Epel, Chronicle Books, 1998.

The Pocket Muse: Ideas & Inspirations for Writing by Monica Wood, Writer's Digest Books, 2002.

The Price of a Gift: A Lakota Healer's Story by Gerald Mohatt and Joseph Eagle Elk, University of Lincoln Press, 2000.

The Prophet by Kahlil Gibran, Alfred A. Knopf, 1999.

Pure Land Haiku: The Art of Priest Issa by David G. Lanoue, Buddhist Books International, 2004. (Also see David's Web site: haikuguy.com.)

The Sea Accepts All Rivers and Other Poems by Judy Sorum Brown, Miles River Press, 2000.

The Search for the Real Self by James F. Masterson, M.D., Simon & Schuster, 1998.

The Selected Poems of Wendell Berry, Counterpoint, 1998.

Step Lightly: Poems for the Journey, compiled by Nancy Willard, HarcourtBrace, 1998.

The Sweet and Sour Animal Book by Langston Hughes, Oxford Press, 1969.

Training the Mind and Cultivating Loving Kindness by Chogya Trungpa, Shambhala Publications, 1993.

The Way It Is: New & Selected Poems by William Stafford, Graywolf Press, 1998.

Thorsons Principles of Native American Spirituality by Timothy Freke and Dennis Renault, Thorsons, 1996.

What Do We Know by Mary Oliver, Perseus Books, 2001.

A Writer's Book of Days by Judy Reeves, New World Library, 1999.

Writing Down the Bones: Freeing the Writer Within by Natalie Goldberg, Shambhala, 1986.

Books of Related Interest

The Thundering Years
Rituals and Sacred Wisdom for Teens
by Julie Tallard Johnson

Teen Psychic
Exploring Your Intuitive Spiritual Powers
by Julie Tallard Johnson

I Ching for Teens
Take Charge of Your Destiny with the Ancient Chinese Oracle
by Julie Tallard Johnson

Teen Dream Power
Unlock the Meaning of Your Dreams
by M. J. Abadie

Teen Feng Shui
Design Your Space, Design Your Life
by Susan Levitt

Awakening to Animal Voices
A Teen Guide to Telepathic Communication with All Life
by Dawn Baumann Brunke

The Goddess in Every Girl
Develop Your Teen Feminine Power
by M. J. Abadie

Teen Astrology
The Ultimate Guide to Making Your Life Your Own
by M. J. Abadie

Inner Traditions • Bear & Company
P.O. Box 388
Rochester, VT 05767
1-800-246-8648
www.InnerTraditions.com

Or contact your local bookseller